# THE LINCOLN ZOO REBELLION

SPEAKING VOLUMES, LLC
NAPLES, FLORIDA
2024

The Lincoln Zoo Rebellion

Copyright © 2024 by Davina Belling and Art Twain

All rights reserved. No part of this book may be reproduced or transmitted in any form or by any means without written permission.

Cover art and illustrations by Vargocie

ISBN 979-8-89022-036-3

# The Lincoln Zoo Rebellion

Larry Belling with Art Twain

The Lincoln Zoo Rebellion is dedicated to young readers—ages eight to fourteen—and to *all* young at heart readers. It gives you a fulfilling reading experience consistent with the expanded world of information that now shapes our lives.

May the child in each of us live a long and rewarding existence.

## Acknowledgments

We, the authors of The Lincoln Zoo Rebellion, want to thank our agent, Nancy Rosenfeld, for her great enthusiasm and dedication in helping to bring this book to the perfect publisher. We thank Kurt and Erica Mueller of Speaking Volumes Publishing for making the publishing of this book such a joyous experience.

We thank Vargocie, whose cover art and internal illustrations sprinkled magic on our literary offering. Her wonderful imagination and boundless creativity has been a blessing.

We especially thank Davina Belling, wife of Larry Belling, for her encouragement, advice, and support throughout the process of writing and helping to bring this book to completion.

Finally, we thank YOU, our readers. You are the most important destination of our journey.

We hope our book gives you a new appreciation of Creatures, whether domesticated, in the wild, or in the Zoos.

After all, we're related. We're all Animals.

## Chapter One

    *The huge male Lion and the old zookeeper raced up the small grassy hill behind the cornfields and into a fringe of poplar trees to the east of the town of Clint East Woods—named after a famous movie star. The sun had just gone behind the distant hills, creating long shadows across the ground. Reggie, the zookeeper, was hardly out of breath, despite his advanced age.*

"Can you smell the meat yet, Goliath?" Reggie asked the Lion.

Goliath, his thick mane rustling with every step, glared at the old man and growled angrily. To most people, Goliath came off as a ferocious looking beast. He had an ample mane, huge teeth (sometimes red with the blood of his dinner), and squinty little eyes that seemed to say, "I want to eat you!" His confident manner of walking looked more like a swagger.

"No! I can't smell it yet!" Goliath said, neither in English nor Lion Language, but rather by sending the words with his mind. The zookeeper understood perfectly.

"Why don't you sniff around that oak tree?" Reggie answered in the same mind language, as he pointed his finger at a nearby Oak tree. "Maybe I hid your dinner out there, heh, heh."

Goliath sauntered up to the tree and sniffed around. Then he reached his huge front paws high on the trunk and hoisted himself up to the first branches. But he couldn't find a scent. "I'm getting tired of these games," Goliath growled impatiently.

"You think your cousins in the wild just sit around, waiting for some poor fool of a zookeeper to plop down a hunk of steak in front of them? No way, Jose!"

"That shows you how much you know," Goliath snorted. "My cousins in the wild have female mates who go out and hunt for their dinner. They eat, they sleep, they hang out, and they don't have to run up dumb hills because some old nut job of a zookeeper enjoys playing childish hide-and-seek games with their food."

Just then, Goliath spotted two young boys with BB guns sneaking around the woods, apparently looking for small animals to torment. The old zookeeper didn't notice the mischief-makers, *though he knew them quite well. The boys, Little Max Flommock and Bobby Winkleman, were better known around town as "the devilish duo." Little Max had bright red-orange hair, which accounted for his nickname, "Carrot Top," and had, according to his pal, Bobby, over ten thousand freckles. His teeth were badly in need of a dentist's attention. In contrast, Bobby's hair was cut so short, he looked almost bald. His father insisted he go to a barber every week and, as he put it, "Git yer ears lowered."*

*Goliath teased Reggie, telling him in mind-talk that he was now stalking fresh prey.*

*"That's a laugh," Reggie answered in fluent Lion-talk. "You wouldn't know real prey if it stuck its tongue out right in front of you."*

*The boys, from their hidden spot in the woods, heard the guttural roaring sounds of Reggie's Lion-talk. It actually sounded more human than any animal sound. Little Max peeked through the trees and recognized Reggie, as he leaned against a tree stump.*

*"I see you, Reggie! How ya doin'?" he lisped through his crooked teeth.*

*Reggie looked around but couldn't see the boy because of the dark shadows in the bushes. "Can't you see us? We're hiding pretty good, eh?" Bobby Winkleman said.*

*Suddenly, Reggie realized that Goliath was actually stalking the two boys, just as he would have done in the wilds of the African savannah, where his ancestors ruled the land.*

*Unlike most of the children of Lincoln, Reggie had no particular fondness for these boys. In fact, when they began coming to the zoo after school, he had taken an extreme dislike* to them. Little Max and Bobby seemed to have no respect whatsoever for the feelings of the animals.

Once they threw lit firecrackers into the cage of Milt, the Tiger, creating three sudden, loud explosions. Milt had yelped hysterically and chased around in circles after his scalded tail. The zookeeper sternly reprimanded the boys and they agreed to behave, which didn't last very long.

Only a week later, Bobby brought a box of moldy vegetables from the dumpster behind his father's grocery store. He and Little Max shoved the box into the Monkeys' cages, who gleefully ate the rotten veggies and became quite ill. Reggie threatened to ban both boys from the zoo but, again, they apologized and promised to be good.

"Don't you think we can behave ourselves, Reggie?" asked Little Max in a smart-alecky way. "Me and Bobby are certainly having a great time!"

"It would be more proper to say, 'Bobby and I' are certainly having a good time!'" Reggie corrected.

Little Max scratched his head. "But it's me and Bobby."

"'Bobby and I' is proper English. You don't say 'me is having good time,' do you? No! You say 'I am having a good time. Bobby and I are having a good time.'"

"Me and Bobby," Little Max shot back defiantly.

Despite his dislike for the boys, Reggie had no desire to see them become Goliath's dinner, which would create a major uproar, shut down the zoo, and put him out of work forever. "You kids had better hurry out of those bushes right this second and come over here to me for protection," he called out.

Their reaction was predictable. The boys just laughed. "Protection against what?" laughed Little Max.

*"Listen to me, you nincompoops..." Reggie yelled. But it was too late.*

*Goliath emerged from behind the trees, bounding towards the boys, with his enormous yellow teeth glistening with drool and his eyes beady and vicious.*

*Suddenly, the boys spotted the Lion and froze, petrified with fear, unable to move a muscle.*

*With a roar, Goliath leaped and soared, floating as if in slow motion right at them with his mouth wide open...*

*"No! No!" Reggie shouted...*

"No! No!" Reggie Goodenough bolted upright in his bed in his cottage on the grounds of Lincoln Zoo, suddenly fully awake, his eyes wide with surprise, his forehead dripping with perspiration.

He'd been dreaming!

And the darned dream felt real, probably because everything and everybody in it *was* real.

"Whew, that was a close one!" Reggie groaned aloud.

It took a full minute for his heavy breathing to calm down. Then he slid off the bed and opened the window he had built into his roof and shouted to the world outside, "It's a zoo out there!"

A Flamingo named Cosmo and a Peahen screeched and squawked in agreement while an ornery Rooster crowed his regular morning, cockamamie "COCKADOODLE DOO!" A small flock of Penguins peeped and brayed. They had mysteriously appeared at the zoo one night and Reggie never found out how they had gotten there. Had someone dropped them off? And why would they do that? Always thinking of what was best for animals, Reggie transported them to Veronica Lake, up in the hills, thinking they would be happier around water. But they kept coming back to the zoo.

Reggie stretched and yawned, and his old bones crackled and popped into place. He slept in an oversized seven-foot bed on a sleeping platform he had built himself above his living room, right up near the ceiling. He had installed a skylight window in the sloping roof. Most nights, before going to sleep, he would place a mug of hot milk on the windowsill and sit up in bed with his head sticking out in the fresh evening air, listening to the sounds of his animals while gazing up at the stars and planets.

He rolled out of bed, slipped on his furry green bedroom slippers, and climbed down the rickety steps of the sleeping platform to the living-room. "If I don't mend these steps, I might fall over on my rear end one day," he would frequently say, but he never seemed to find the time to fix the darn things.

Fast asleep on the couch in his living room lay a Ring-tailed Lemur from the island of Madagascar named Louie. Reggie woke the snoring Lemur, who meowed like a cat, as Lemurs do, bidding Reggie 'good morning.' Reggie meowed back in Lemur language that Louie had better hightail it back to his cage, which he promptly did with his tail held high.

Reggie then went into his kitchen and turned on the gas of his old black iron stove. He lit the flame and put on the kettle. The night before, as he did every night, he had filled it with his special blend of peppermint and spearmint teas. He grew the mint himself in his greenhouse. It was a favorite of a small group of children who came to visit him at the zoo most afternoons after school.

In his bathroom, the old zookeeper examined his craggy face in the mirror.

*Grrrrr!* he grimaced at himself. *Maybe I ought to stay in bed all day.* He combed his snow-white handlebar mustache and full head of riotous hair, which seemed to come out of his head like electric wires. Surprisingly, his eyebrows were bushy and jet black without even a trace of grey. Two of his mother's close friends, Sadie and Tiny Teeny—who were old enough to be great-grandmothers and lived at a retirement home nearby—once tried to spread a rumor that he put shoe polish on his bushy brows, but thankfully no one believed them.

The kettle in the kitchen began squealing with its urgent, high-pitched whine, signaling the animals outside to explode into a chorus of wake-up noises that rumbled and thundered through the morning air. The animals knew the piercing sound of that kettle meant their breakfast would soon be on its way. Reggie recognized the peculiar roar of Milt the Tiger.

"Hold onto your stripes!" Reggie yelled. "I've got to brush my teeth!" He squeezed out a huge gob of toothpaste and brushed vigorously. Then, he jumped into his overalls, gulped down the hot peppermint tea, and scurried out the back door.

Beyond the greenhouse sat a large red barn, where the animals' food was stored. Inside the barn, Reggie selected meat from the walk-in refrigerator, because the carnivores were always fed first, and loaded it onto his wheelbarrow. Carnivores are animals who eat mainly meat and, although Reggie ate no meat himself, he recognized that nature made certain animals in a way that meat was the only food that kept them healthy.

"Goliath!" Reggie roared in Lion language, "Come and get it!"

The Lion laughed his great Lion laugh. "That was one fantastical dream you had last night, Reggie," he roared in his distinctive East African dialect.

Reggie had been astonished to discover that the Lion had been able to see the old zookeeper's dreams, as if they were movies. The only other animal who could ever do that was a Canadian Red Fox named Hugh.

"I just wish you didn't wake up at the best moment!" roared the Lion.

"It was a silly dream," Reggie replied. "You never jumped that high or that far in your entire life. A Puma can leap in the air, but the only African Lions with that ability are the females." Goliath knew that the Puma was a smaller American cousin of the Lions, sometimes called a Cougar or Mountain Lion. He loved that Reggie was so full of interesting animal facts.

"I have to admit it," mumbled Goliath. "I'm seriously challenged in the jumping department."

Reggie pushed a nine-pound hunk of steak through the bars to the delighted Goliath, who picked it up in his gaping mouth and tossed it into the air. It landed on the cement floor with a thud. Goliath pounced on it and commenced ripping it to shreds. He always played with his food before actually eating it.

Reggie watched him with amusement, but also with a hint of sadness in his eyes. He remembered a time not very long before when he and his animals really did play hide-and-seek with their food in the hills above Lincoln, known as the Horace Heights. He would drive an ancient electric golf cart filled with a large container of food and place it in various places among the trees, bushes, and ponds. Then he'd signal the animals to come find their meals, using their keen natural senses of smell and sight. They loved doing that.

There were no houses up there yet and his animals could run around as much as they wanted. In those days, the noisiest sound was the screeching call of Blue Jays and the honking of Canada Geese on their way back home after their migration to sunnier climates. During the corn-planting season, the animals had to endure the awful aroma of fertilizer. But now the cornfields were gone. Sadly, as far as the zoo life was concerned, all the farms around Lincoln and the public woodlands had disappeared and a modern new city had sprung to life with apartment buildings, tract houses, shopping malls, and schools.

New roads were built, and a government worker, Magnus Pittypat, was put in charge of naming them. Magnus was an avid movie fan, so it was no surprise that he named the streets after famous old movie stars, such as Humphrey Bogart and Spencer Tracy, as well as newer ones: Brad Pitt Way, Jennifer Lawrence Lane, DiCaprio Road, and Meryl Streep Street. Lincoln quickly filled up with cars and trucks bringing goods and food from other places.

At the center of Lincoln towered the spanking new, block-long Throttlebottom Toy Factory, an enterprise that brought thousands of workers to the town, huge amounts of money for new development...and misery to the old zookeeper, Reggie, who longed for the good old days of his animals' freedom.

With all that construction, the zoo withered. Animals were forced to spend more time in their cages. To Reggie, it seemed like he was running the incredible shrinking zoo.

And soon things would become even worse.

## Chapter Two

Ralph Throttlebottom, a red-faced man with a bulbous nose and an enormous belly, finished his breakfast: a half dozen scrambled eggs topped with a particularly stinky, soft, cow's milk cheese (aka: Limburger cheese), and onions, drowning in Tabasco sauce on pumpernickel bread, washed down by a huge mug of cappuccino. He belched loudly, making his wife, Libby, cringe.

Throttlebottom's breath smelled rather toxic, so he pulled out a silver flask which contained spearmint mouthwash, took a big sip, threw back his head, gargled noisily, and spit it out—right into his empty cappuccino mug. Libby sighed at his lack of manners but was thankful he seldom did it when they dined out at restaurants.

"We've been so busy building my toy factory, I've never even seen the zoo in this here dumpy town. I think I'll take a spin over there," Throttlebottom mused.

Can I come too?" Libby asked.

"No, it's business," he replied.

"Well, if you meet a veterinarian, ask him what I should do about Princess Mookie's claws. She ripped up three pillows in the guest room." Mookie was the Throttlebottom's white Persian Cat, who hated them both.

The Throttlebottoms lived in a ten-room mansion that Ralph had recently built in the shape of a castle, with turrets and a shallow moat filled with murky water. The property was quite enormous, with a separate garage, tennis court, and swimming pool. Strangely enough, Throttlebottom and his wife didn't play tennis or enjoy swimming, even during the hot summer months, nor did they have any children who might wish to do so.

Throttlebottom, a rather fat man, waddled out the front door of the fake castle and walked towards the garage. His three Cadillac stretch limousines were nicely lined up, ready to go. He chose the red one, climbed inside, and set off for the zoo, breaking every speed limit, despite the fact that he was not in a hurry.

He pulled the huge car through the gates of the zoo and screeched to a halt right in the middle of the Kentucky blue grass lawn in front of Reggie's cottage. Reggie looked out the window in horror.

"Please do not park there!" he called out. *Hmph! Who is this road hog of a person?* he asked himself.

The electric windows of the Cadillac rolled down and Throttlebottom stuck his head out of the window. "Howdy, old timer," he yelled. "I am Mister Throttlebottom of the famous toy company. Who the blazes are you?"

"I'm Reggie Goodenough, the head zookeeper, and I would prefer if you would park your exceptionally large vehicle on the dirt path over there instead of on this lawn, which I personally planted."

"Gee, I'm sorry, Pops!" Throttlebottom hollered. "I didn't notice the grass." He promptly moved his car onto the pathway. "Where's the veterinarian?" Throttlebottom shouted, getting out of the car. "I need some advice about my wife's Persian Pussycat."

"We don't have a vet," Reggie replied as calmly as he could muster. "All my animals are as healthy as they can be. Would you care to take a look at some of them?"

"Yeah, okay," grumbled Throttlebottom, glancing at his watch, "But I don't have much time."

After mind-projecting to the animals to be on their very best behavior, Reggie showed Throttlebottom around the zoo. The fat man's face became a snooty grin as he quickly viewed the spotless cages that Reggie had spent time decorating with plants and trees from the animals' original homes in the wild.

He saw the pens of Adolf and Sigmund, the Crocodile and Alligator. He breezed by the cage of Milt, the Tiger, with hardly a glance at the beautifully striped feline. He peeked at the Hippo's enclosure, but saw nothing, since Rambo was submerged in his pool. Always in a hurry, Throttlebottom didn't take the time to wait for the four-ton hulk of Rambo to rise.

Reggie had difficulty holding back his laughter when Leslie Wolf barked out, "That guy looks like a giant Wild Boar!"

"Not bad, old man!" Throttlebottom said with gusto as they returned to the cottage, "But it's pretty small for a growing town like Lincoln. Tell you what I'm gonna do. When I win the election for mayor, I'll build this zoo into a showplace, 'cause I am going to be the best mayor anyone has ever seen in the history of mayors!"

Reggie wondered why Throttlebottom talked so loudly. It suddenly came to him that the man assumed, since Reggie was of a certain advanced age, that he was probably deaf, not realizing that Reggie could hear an Antelope snoring a half a mile away.

Suddenly, Reggie saw this as his chance to inform Throttlebottom of his desire for a better, more open zoo. With more funds, the old zookeeper could arrange displays that would better show how animals *actually* live in the wild: environments called "habitats." Perhaps he could even arrange for mates for the younger animals. That would be wonderful! Goliath was particularly lonely, and Milt the Tiger was even lonelier.

Reggie had often dreamed of a zoo where the animals lived completely separated from visitors by rivers or small lakes. "Let's stick the *human animals* in cages!" he would exclaim to his mother's lady friends, Tiny Teeny and Sadie, at the Bedside Manor Retirement Home.

Reggie began talking excitedly to Throttlebottom of his dreams for a better zoo. "We could make marvelous improvements. We could turn it into a breeding zoo and supply animals to other zoos." The words spilled out of his mouth so rapidly that Throttlebottom feared the old man would have a heart seizure.

"Calm down, Pops!" he shouted. "I catch your drift! When I'm elected mayor, I'm going to raise enough money to do some really special things with this zoo that will bring lots of tourist dollars to Lincoln! I see you know your apples, so you'll hear from me before any major decisions are made. Say old timer, how old are you anyway?"

Reggie was reluctant to reveal his true age in case Throttlebottom thought he was too old for the job. "I was born when there were fewer zoos and a lot more animals in the wild," Reggie winked at Throttlebottom, hoping the potential mayor-to-be would take his response as playful chat, and not as trying to avoid telling his age.

Though that wasn't the answer that Throttlebottom wanted, he let the matter pass and got back into his car. He took the top off the silver flask sitting on the passenger seat, took a mouthful of spearmint mouthwash, sloshed it around noisily, then spit it out the window (splashing Reggie's shoe), and drove off down the path, running over a bed of pansies.

Reggie didn't know whether to be encouraged or discouraged by Throttlebottom's visit. On one hand, the man seemed to be listening when Reggie spoke about habitats and mates for the animals. But there was a nagging doubt. "Anyone who yells at old people because he thinks they are deaf, hasn't thought things through properly," he murmured to himself.

Reggie wandered over to the enclosure of Sam, the Giraffe. Sam bent his eight-foot neck down until his small face was eyeball-to-eyeball with Reggie. He told Sam about his visit with the toy king. Since Giraffes have no vocal cords, Reggie communicated mostly with his mind, but also with a few quiet squeaks, tsks and moos.

"I don't much like what he's done to this town," he telepathed to Sam. "Also, he's a pretty rotten road-hog of a driver and he spits! I certainly don't think I'll vote for him for Mayor, but I have to admit his toys look pretty good."

Throttlebottom Toys sold in every top toy shop across America. Their specialty was stuffed animals, but they also made board games, dolls, model cars, and trains.

Their toy Bear, named "Ralph" after Throttlebottom himself, was modeled on the Kodiak Brown Bear, one of the largest land carnivores in the world. Because it was made to look realistic, Reggie believed it taught young children more about real Bears than the usual cartoon-style, Teddies. He also liked their Willie Wombat, but it didn't sell nearly as well as the Bears did.

The toy factory brought a seething mass of construction to the town of Lincoln. There was little time to build houses for the new workers, so 180 prefabricated homes were brought in on trucks, plunked down on a vacant piece of land near Veronica Lake and before you could say "Robinson Crusoe," the families moved in.

Other businesses followed: laundries, beauty salons, coffee shops, restaurants, drug stores, and a movie theatre opened for business. Two new churches and a synagogue were built, and the local television station's transmitter was upgraded to cover a larger area. A new school was constructed: Barack Obama Middle School. Little Max and Bobby enrolled there as did other local children who often visited the zoo, including Cory Chang, Jaime Gutierrez, LaToya Tricklebank, Melly Belloso and Scooter Goldfarb.

After all that construction, the biggest change that Reggie noticed was the noise of the cars. For the first time there were traffic jams, exhaust fumes, and horns honking. Magnus Pittypat, who had the task of choosing street names, ran out of movie stars so he decided to name the streets after parts of the body: Funny Bone Street, Ankle Avenue, Nostril Way, Kneecap Lane, Elbow Place, Ribcage Road, and Belly Button Boulevard. The road to the zoo, however, remained "Lincoln Zoo Road."

A used car lot, "Big Max's Steals n' Deals" on Nostril Way was opened by Little Max's father, Max Flommock, a newcomer from Peanut, California. A major gas station was built by an extremely nervous businessman named Howard Plitt, who had moved to Lincoln from Truth or Consequences, New Mexico. Bill Winkleman, Bobby's father, opened his third grocery store there.

Although the toy factory was good for Lincoln, it added to air pollution, both by the increase of traffic and, especially at five o'clock in the afternoon, when remnants of fabric too small to be useful in manufacturing stuffed animals were burned. Huge puffs of yellow smoke billowed from the chimney. *I wonder what's in that gunk that makes my eyes turn red and my mustache twitch?* Reggie often asked himself.

It turned out that Throttlebottom had no need for Reggie's vote to become mayor. He was elected by a landslide. All the toy factory workers voted for him because they were afraid that they might lose their jobs if he found out they *didn't* vote for him. Prominent people in Lincoln, including the bank president and owner of the insurance company, threw their support behind him because Throttlebottom allowed them to play on his tennis court and swim in his pool.

Throttlebottom's first action as mayor was to appoint a City Council, which immediately agreed to his demands to waive all sales taxes on his toy store, as well as property taxes on his factory, and even his mock castle, which he claimed would be used as a special office.

The City Council also agreed to the mayor's demands to impose a tax to improve the zoo. It required that each adult had to pay two dollars a week (deducted from his or her salary) and schoolchildren had to pay fifty cents a week out of their lunch money. Even Reggie had to pay the zoo tax, which he thought was ridiculous considering his modest salary.

The City Council also appointed a Board of Directors for the zoo. Throttlebottom demanded that he himself should be appointed Chairman of the Board because of his special understanding of big financial projects. Used car dealer, Big Max Flommock, was appointed president; Grocery store owner, Bill Winkleman, became vice-president; and Howard Plitt from the new gas station was selected secretary-treasurer.

Within a year, a considerable sum of money had piled up from the zoo tax and an announcement appeared in the Sunday *Lincoln Examiner* that Mayor Throttlebottom was going to make a special important announcement Wednesday night on Lincoln's local Channel Three television news. He commanded everyone to tune in.

# The Lincoln Zoo Rebellion

Reggie rode his bicycle over to the Bedside Manor Retirement Home to watch the program with his friends, Sadie and Tiny Teeny, since he had no TV set of his own. Sadie always offered him a snack of dried apricots, which he enjoyed, but Tiny Teeny couldn't eat them because they got stuck to her false teeth. Tiny Teeny didn't have a real tooth in her entire mouth.

First the news was read by Bernie Moon, a twenty-seven-year-old local boy whose dream of appearing on TV had finally come true in the form of his very own TV show, which he hosted. His main job, however, was staff reporter for the *Lincoln Examiner.* Moon could write very quickly, but didn't always check his facts thoroughly, and often jumped to conclusions.

For instance, he once interviewed Reggie about animals of different species that could live together in harmony. Reggie started to explain about animals' *compatibility,* but Moon thought he said *pet-ability.* So, Moon immediately jumped to the wrong conclusion that if you pet animals of various species frequently, all would be well. He wrote this nonsense in his column.

Moon had a mop of curly hair, a big wide smile, and a full round face. Tiny Teeny, with her false teeth going clickety-click, loved to say, "He's Moon by name and Moon by face!"

After Moon finished reading the news about a traffic accident to his TV audience, he plunked the script papers down into a neat stack and looked directly at the camera.

"And now," he intoned in his deepest voice, "I take great pleasure in presenting the mayor of our town of Lincoln and Chairman of the Board of the zoo, Mr. Ralph Throttlebottom."

The Mayor beamed from ear to ear. "People of Lincoln, rejoice!" he bellowed. "We have raised enough money from the zoo tax to make additions to our crummy old zoo that will make it the coolest, most entertaining, amusing, and fabulously fun zoo in these United States!"

Reggie turned to Sadie. "Cool? Fun? Entertaining? What in the world is he talking about?"

Throttlebottom continued. "We will be adding a giant swimming pool, a merry-go-round, a bowling alley, a video game arcade with a real shooting gallery, and the best toy store money can buy; run, of course, by the Throttlebottom Toy Company!"

Reggie couldn't believe his ears. "What poppycock!" he cried. "Bowling? Merry-go-round? Those things don't belong at zoos! *Animals* belong at zoos! What the heck is a video game arcade anyway?"

"Moreover," Throttlebottom proclaimed, "we have asked Governor Gladstone at the state capital if he would support legislation that would allow us to build a fabulous gambling casino and hotel adjoining the zoo, so when people got tired of looking at animals they could go and try to win their fortunes!"

"What a load of malarkey!" gasped Reggie with disbelief. "Gambling here in Lincoln? I think I'm going to barf!"

Throttlebottom gave a 'thumbs up' sign. "Yes! Starting next Thursday, the zoo will be closed to the public and construction work will begin. The new, improved zoo will open three months from Saturday with great festivities! And furthermore, since it is sort of a zoo after all, we're gonna get us some new, really fine, giant animals from Central Africa. I already ordered them by e-mail."

Reggie jumped out of his chair and barked a particularly naughty curse word in Spider Monkey, which sounded something like 'GRWANGRES!' He punched the power button on the TV set and the mayor's face disappeared. Tiny Teeny and Sadie rose from the couch and came over to hug him.

"New giant animals?" Reggie moaned. "What kind of animals? What happened to his promise to consult me? This, my dear ladies, is the beginning of real trouble!"

## Chapter Three

"Jobi" Conn O'Brien, a craggy-faced, blond-haired former game tracker, stomped on the gas pedal of his Zebra-striped Land Rover jeep as the vehicle skidded around on the bumpy dirt road in the Central African savannah. "Hang on!" he cried. With a roar of the engine, the jeep caught hold and took off towards a fast-running baby Elephant.

The vehicle backfired noisily as it bounced over rain-filled potholes. In the back seat, Peter Nelson N'gara, a super-smart thirteen year-old, clung to the overhead railing for dear life. Behind them, a khaki-colored open truck followed nearby in hot pursuit, as the baby Elephant's protector, an elderly rogue male Elephant, thundered at nearly his top speed of twenty-five miles per hour, trumpeting his distress and anger. Considered a "rogue" because he didn't mix with other Elephants, but was an outcast, traveling and living alone, his advanced age slowed him down a bit. But adrenalin allowed him to overcome his exhaustion.

Following the old rogue, seven Rhodesian Ridgeback Dogs successfully completed their job of cutting him off from the baby. But the canines were getting tired and losing ground.

Jobi Conn's number one man, Joe Otoronga, sat behind the wheel of the speeding open truck, with his three African helpers, Kafi, Evaristo and Mitch, bouncing around on the loading platform behind. Two of the men carried rifles, but Jobi Conn had very strict rules that anyone who fired a weapon at an animal without being in mortal danger would lose his job immediately. *Jobi* means "boss" in the Swahili language and Conn O'Brien, despite his lack of book learning, was terrific at his job. When Jobi Conn gave an order, his workers paid close attention.

The baby Elephant turned right. Joe Otoronga swerved the steering wheel to the right. The baby Elephant turned left. Joe quickly pulled his wheel to the left. The old rogue was dropping behind, exhausted and emotional at the prospect of separation from the baby. The baby Elephant's mother had been killed by poachers a few weeks earlier, and the old rogue had committed to doing his best to protect it from harm. Elephants are very family oriented and protective toward their species.

Finally, the baby suddenly slowed down, then stopped running, and stood still, trying to catch its breath. The four men quickly jumped out of the truck and let down the tailgate. One of them grabbed the baby's trunk, the other three pushed from behind, and in a few minutes the baby Elephant was tied to the railing and on her way to a large wildlife rescue division of the Central African Mbinguni Rescue Reserve, run by Jobi Conn, who catered to protecting and healing sick, injured, and orphaned animals. Mbinguni means "heaven" in Swahili, and this reserve was certainly heaven for the animals being cared for and rehabilitated in the reserve. Jobi Conn then sent many of the recovered animals that might otherwise end up as targets for poachers to the safety of zoos around the world. (They also used to supply them to circuses, but thank goodness, that type of animal cruelty is a thing of the past.) Nowadays, zoos got their animals from reserves like the Mbinguni and from other zoos through their breeding programs.

The old rogue elephant, physically and emotionally exhausted, gave up his chase. Sides heaving with loud, whooshing breaths, he ambled slowly in the same direction as the moving truck. Peter thought he detected a sad look in his age-weary Elephant eyes, as it watched the baby disappear in the swirling dust in the distance.

Jobi Conn, in the Land Rover, doubled back to collect the Dogs, which clambered up into the vehicle, panting with deep, wet breaths. Jobi Conn turned north.

"Don't you feel sorry for the old rogue?" Peter asked timidly, his young mind filled with compassion.

"Of course I do, old bean!" Jobi Conn answered. He called men he liked "old bean," a British expression meaning "buddy" or "friend," and even though Peter was only thirteen, Jobi Conn considered him to be a grown-up after all the troubles the boy had been through.

"But the old rogue is used to being alone. And more important, he is too old to take care of this baby Elephant. Without a mother, the poor little guy will either starve or become a meal for predators. I think it's better for the little fella to have a nice safe life in a zoo, especially with all these criminal poachers running around murdering Elephants for their ivory tusks."

"But why can't you send a healthy grown-up Elephant, like Blomm, to a zoo, rather than a baby?" Peter asked. Blomm was a full-grown male who had been at the reserve for more than a year.

"Ah, he's a problem, that one is," Jobi Conn answered. "A poacher who was hiding at the edge of a river shot his gun at Blomm and grazed his leg. The poacher then slipped on a rock and fell into the river. Blomm ran right over, picked up the gun and smashed it to bits against a tree. We caught him a few hours later and nursed him back to health, but I've been reluctant to send him off to a zoo."

"Why is that?" asked Peter.

"'Cause every time he sees a gun of any sort, or even someone carrying a long stick, or even a cane, he goes crazy! You've never heard such carryings-on in your entire life!"

When they got back to camp, Peter stopped by to see the Blomm. The elephant looked at him suspiciously. Then Peter put out his hand, holding a shiny green apple, but Blomm turned away. Disappointed, Peter dropped the apple and went to his tent. Soon after he had gone, Blomm plucked the apple from the ground, stuffed it in his mouth and ate the whole thing with one great chew and a gulp.

Jobi Conn sat on the verandah of his white-painted house and relaxed after his tough day of chasing Elephants. His blonde hair was matted and his safari jacket damp with sweat. His houseboy had poured him a large glass of whisky and he was about to take a sip when Joe Otoronga came running from the communications shed.

## The Lincoln Zoo Rebellion

"You got an e-mail on the computer in the office all the way from America, Jobi Conn! It looks like money in da bank!" Joe thrust the e-mail printout into Jobi Conn's hands. It read as follows:

*From: mayor@thelincolnzoo.org*
*To: Jobi Conn O'Brien. Central African Mbinguni Game Reserve.*

*Urgent rush animal order needed three months from Saturday.*
*Please dispatch really big Leopard, Yellow Baboon, Spotted Hyena, Aardvark, Elephant with extra big ears, Black Rhino, Wildebeest, Giant Anteater, Wart Hog, Pygmy Chimpanzee, Thompson's Gazelle, Ostrich, Okapi, Mountain Gorilla and variety assortment Snakes and Lizards. We are in a big hurry for these animals. We will pay top dollar.*
*Ralph Throttlebottom. Mayor. Chairman, Board of Lincoln Zoo.*

"Does this guy think I'm nuts?" Jobi Conn sneered, balling up the paper and tossing it on the deck of the verandah. "Nobody could fill that order in less than a year!"

"But Jobi," Joe implored, "we got lots of mouths to feed 'round here. This looks like a pretty good way to get a lot of money in a short time. Why not let me spread the word among the other reserves and some zoos and see what they can come up with? Maybe we can round up some animals in record time."

"I can always count on you, Joe. I love your optimism. There must be plenty of healthy animals on the list scattered around other reserves that would be perfect for the zoo. When they rehabilitate injured or sick or orphaned animals, they can't always just put them back out into the wild. Especially with the growing number of poachers."

"Yes, Jobi. Many people think that it's easy to just push healthy animals back into the wild. But that's not always possible. And the zoos with breeding programs make new babies that take up more room than they have. So a new zoo is the perfect new home for them."

"Okay, Joe, old bean," Jobi Conn sipped his whisky. "but I ain't makin' no promises to some stupid mayor who doesn't even know that Anteaters come from South America! Give me a piece of paper and I'll draft an e-mail to send back to him."

Peter had decided to take a little nap before dinner, after the exhaustion of the long day. He lay on his cot, but he couldn't sleep, thinking about his parents and where they might be.

Two months before, his mother, Lakeisha, and his father, Seko, had been snatched from their home in the middle of the night by the secret police who worked for the dictator president of their small Central African country, Mbinguni. Peter's father, a trained lawyer, had been appointed Minister of Tourism, and did a superb job of attracting tourists to the area.

But when a newspaper wrote about the mysterious disappearance of several tourists at an expensive mountain lodge, visitors cancelled their plans to visit the country. Tourism revenues crashed, people lost their jobs and there was an uprising against the dictator accusing him of corruption.

Unfortunately, the dictator placed the blame directly on Peter's father. He ordered the police to go to the home of the N'gara family and arrest them and throw them in jail. But the night they came to do their dastardly deed, Peter, their only child, had gone to stay overnight at the house of a school friend.

The next day, he returned home, completely unaware that anything was wrong. He ran up the drive and opened the front door and his eyes grew wide with surprise and fear.

The living room was completely bare! Where did the furniture go? The hardwood floors so recently covered with finely woven rugs were littered with garbage. The family pictures on the walls were now just darkened squares on the wallpaper.

Peter didn't know what to do. He went from room to room in shock. The telephones had been ripped from the walls. The refrigerator and stove were missing from the kitchen. The cupboards had been cleaned out, except for two lonely cans of lima beans and a few loose groundnuts (which we call peanuts). Everything was gone, including his clothes and his schoolbooks.

He sat on the floor of his barren room and wondered what he should do. He thought about calling some relatives in Nairobi, many hundreds of miles away in East Africa, but he was afraid to leave the house.

Late in the afternoon, he heard the sound of a car driving up and down the street. Suddenly, a loudspeaker blared an announcement that sent chills up his spine.

"Anyone knowing the whereabouts of the boy, Peter Nelson N'gara, is ordered to come out onto the street immediately."

The car stopped in front of his house and he peeked out the window. Four men in tan safari suits got out of the car and started up the drive. Peter ran to the closet of his bedroom, hoisted himself up by the clothes bar and removed the wooden trap door. He climbed into the attic hiding place and replaced the panel.

He held his breath as the men searched the vacant house looking for him, but, thankfully, they did not check the attic.

News travels fast in the center of Africa, even to places with poor wifi reception. The word spread quickly about the arrest of Seko and Lakeisha N'gara. Joe Otoronga heard the story from a mail carrier whose route took him by the Mbinguni African Game Reserve headquarters.

"Those people are my second cousins!" he cried. "I must go and rescue little Peter."

Joe borrowed Jobi Conn's Land Rover and rushed into town as fast as it would go. He found the boy in the attic, scared, tired and hungry. Peter had managed to pry open four cans of lima beans, but a few beans and groundnuts were hardly enough for a growing boy to eat for four days.

Joe stopped at a local fast-food joint, bought a huge pizza, and drove a well-fed Peter back to the Game Reserve. Jobi Conn agreed to take him in and support him, as long as Peter helped occasionally around the place. The boy agreed enthusiastically.

"Joe, old bean," Jobi Conn called out, putting down his pencil. "I have written an e-mail for you to send to that zoo mayor in America." Joe took the sheet of paper and read it, shaking his head in doubt.

"He is going to be extremely disappointed, Jobi," Joe cautioned.

"Well, it is very difficult to fill his order within the time frame," Jobi Conn answered. "And besides, he never even offered to send a deposit! Does he think we work for no money? What a fool!"

## Chapter Four

Flommock, Winkleman, and Plitt gathered for their first meeting of the Board of Directors in the conference room of the zoo's new office building, a flimsy structure with red wooden shingles on the roof and walls so thin that a person could hear a toilet flushing in the bathroom next door. Sure enough, the men heard the toilet flush, followed by the sound of gargling and spitting. A minute later, Throttlebottom burst into the room, almost tearing the door from its hinges.

"It's gonna be fantastic!" he exclaimed, putting his silver flask of mouthwash in his pocket. "All the new construction is on time and on budget and this e-mail just arrived!" He held up a print-out. "It must be the good news we've been waiting for." He read the e-mail out loud:

*From: Jobiconn@CAGR.ga*

*Greetings from Africa. Mayor Throttleottom, old bean. Your animal order not possible. It takes extremely long time to locate and secure your list of wild animals. Cannot fill your order in less than one year. Also, no Giant Anteaters in Africa. They live in South America, which is far, far away from here. Mountain Gorillas practically extinct. Cannot send Warthoggies because US government afraid of swine diseases. Sorry about that. By the way, how much deposit are you willing to pay?*
*Jobi Conn O'Brien, Central African Game Reserve.*

"This is outrageous!" thundered Throttlebottom. "He can't do this to us!"

"Ralph! What are we going to do, Ralph?" Flommock blustered. "We can't wait a year, Ralph! Can we Ralph?" Flommock had a fear of forgetting people's names, so he repeated them often, sometimes within the same sentence.

"Of course not!" answered Throttlebottom, banging his pudgy fist on the table. "I'm going to demand that he sends us those animals right now. I promised the people of Lincoln some new animals on my TV broadcast!"

"What do you suggest?" Winkleman asked.

"I'm going to send another e-mail to that Jobi *bird brain* and demand that he transport whatever animals he can as quickly as possible by air freight. He can ship the rest of them later by sea.

## The Lincoln Zoo Rebellion

Throttlebottom grabbed a writing pad and scribbled another message:

*From: mayor@thelincolnzoo.org*

*Dear Mr. Jobi. You must do better. We need animals immediately by air. Forget Anteater and Warthog and substitute any other kind of Gorilla. Send everything else via fastest ship. I am sending you a deposit right away. And stop calling me old bean. I'm Ralph!*

*Ralph Throttlebottom, Mayor.*

He thrust the paper into Flommock's hand. "Get this off immediately!" Big Max Flommock ran out of the room, slamming the door behind him, which opened up a crack on the flimsy wall.

"Now, let's go inspect the progress outside," the mayor ordered.

CRUCHHH! GRECHHH! The bulldozers chewed out great holes of earth for the new main square. PLAMM! RONGGGGCCCHH! The huge machines loaded giant dump trucks with earth in one place, only to be dropped off at some other location nearby. Cranes and equipment vehicles of all sizes and shapes that had arrived a few weeks ago chugged and clanked loudly, while armies of steel workers, welders, carpenters, and masons worked as busy as ants. The directors watched the activity with glee.

The noise and dust of construction around the zoo had become truly horrendous from morning to dusk. Reggie worried mightily about how it would affect his animals.

Buildings seemed to spring up instantaneously on the main square. Besides the flimsy office building, there was the veterinary surgery facility, a shopping mall and, of course, in the most prominent position, the Throttlebottom Toy Store.

"I would have thought offices and toy stores should be located on the outskirts of the zoo," Reggie mentioned to Rambo the Hippo. "And animals should be housed on the main square."

"I really couldn't care less," Rambo yawned. "I just want to get as far away from this racket as possible."

At the entrance to the zoo, ornate wrought-iron gates were installed. The clamor of hammers on metal went on for days. A blacksmith bent iron pipes to spell out 'Lincoln Zoo' and padlocks were welded into place. A mountain of barbed wire was unrolled and stretched all the way around the zoo grounds. Throttlebottom was concerned that people might try to sneak inside without buying an admission ticket.

Reggie thought the barbed wire was a terrible eyesore, not to mention an insult to the honest people of Lincoln. But when he suggested to vice-president Bill Winkleman that they plant tall hedges to hide the wires, Winkleman just laughed right in his face.

"We're not going to spend money on hedges, old timer," Winkleman scoffed. "Bowling alleys are more important!" He and his son Bobby had been traveling fifteen miles to the nearest bowling center to enjoy that activity and were eagerly looking forward to the completion of the zoo's new games center, only a short hop away from home.

Snack bars and soft drink stands popped up everywhere and were painted a hideous orange color. The merry-go-round was shipped in from a bankrupt amusement park in New Jersey. It arrived in over 200 pieces which were dumped alongside Milt the Tiger's cage. The Tiger was bewildered by all the different body parts of painted wooden animals lying on the ground. "They don't smell like animals," he complained.

Reggie promised Milt he would try to move his cage to another location after the merry-go-round was assembled or else the poor Tiger might become dizzy watching the thing go round and round all day long.

With their nightly exercise curtailed, many of the animals exhibited signs of lethargy. They were sleeping longer and sulking around their cages. Reggie tried to visit them more frequently, but they remained groggy and listless.

"How are you feeling," Reggie asked Leslie Wolf one morning when he found the Timber Wolf moping around his splendidly decorated cage. Reggie had imported birch trees and flowers gathered from the woods close to Leslie's birthplace in the Northwest Territories of Canada.

"All this noise is driving me bonkers!" the Wolf exclaimed.

"Of course it's jangling your nerves!" Reggie agreed. "Your hearing is seventeen times more sensitive than us human animals!" Reggie later brought him some earmuffs to dampen the sound. The Wolf looked pretty silly wearing them, but no one noticed. The workers were all too busy with their tasks to pay any attention to the animals.

Although the zoo was closed to the public during construction, Reggie continued to entertain children in his cottage after school. He fed them snacks of peppermint tea, nuts and fruit, and his specialty, snickerdoodles: oatmeal cookies with butter and cinnamon. He tried to impress upon them that the new zoo construction was harming the animals.

"Me and Bobby would rather go visit the men building the new bowling alley," lisped Little Max Flommock through his crooked teeth.

"Surely you mean 'Bobby and I,'" Reggie snapped at him.

Little Max was confused. "Are you saying you want to go with us?"

"Definitely not. It is correct English for you to say, 'Bobby and I want to go.' Not 'me and Bobby.'" Reggie patiently explained. "You wouldn't say 'me go to bed,' would you? Of course not. You would say 'I go to bed,' hence Bobby and I go to the bowling alley."

"I speak American, Reggie," responded Little Max coolly.

Exasperated, Reggie replied, "The animals want you to visit them, young man. I am positively certain they do."

Little Max laughed a mocking laugh. "How do you know that? You ain't no Dr. Doolittle," referring to an imaginary book character who spoke to cartoon animals with silly names like Gub-Gub (a Pig) and Dab-Dab (a Duck).

Reggie shook his head in dismay as the Devilish Duo scurried away, followed by other children, including Cory Chang, Jaime Gutierrez, LaToya Tricklebank, Melly Belloso and Scooter Goldfarb, traveling on his new red action scooter.

He couldn't tell the children that the animals actually told him they were suffering. He had made a promise to himself to never tell anyone about his special skill for animal communication. *People might think I'm a delusional old wackadoodle,* he thought. *They might try to make me appear on TV or that computer thing called a YouTube.*

Occasionally, however, Reggie would tell Sadie and Tiny Teeny something the animals told him. Sadie would nod and smile. Tiny Teeny would say, "That's nice, dear," and her false teeth would rattle. He smiled, knowing they didn't really quite get it.

Besides the irritating construction noise, Reggie was upset by the attitudes of Flommock, Winkleman, and Plitt, who arrived at the zoo every day carrying clipboards and checking off things that needed to be accomplished. The three of them rushed around, scurrying hither and thither, shouting orders at Reggie, each trying to prove to Throttlebottom that he was the busiest and most capable of all his directors.

Max Flommock, the used car dealer, was the most bothersome. He was a tall man with a bad temper and curly red hair like his son Little Max. He made impossible demands on the zookeeper, endlessly asking him to repair things that had broken. Reggie bristled at Flommock's irritating way of speaking.

"Reggie, I want you to go fix the swivel chair in my office, Reggie. It just broke when I sat on it, Reggie. What's your answer, Reggie?"

"Yes, Mr. Flommock," he answered, and then whispered to himself, *I know my own name, you bumbling dorkmeister.*

In the office building, Reggie noticed that several cracks had recently appeared in the ceiling, and the floorboards made strange squeaking sounds. "Not very well constructed," he mumbled. He opened his toolbox, removed a screwdriver and quickly put the swivel chair back together again.

As he was ready to leave the room, he spotted a big red leather book lying on top of the desk. He made out the gold-embossed lettering on the front cover: the word 'Ledger.'

"I haven't seen one of these in years! What a pleasure in this day of computers and plastic to see a good old-fashioned leather ledger. Hey, that almost rhymes in English. It sort of rhymes in Hippo language, too!" But what he saw in the book gave him no pleasure whatsoever.

On the first two pages, the amounts of money spent on the new buildings were listed, and they were enormous! He was shocked to see that the zoo directors, including Throttlebottom himself, were taking supervision fees and there was a huge budget for parties and entertaining. The cost of the video games and video arcade, including the shooting gallery, merry-go-round, shopping mall, and bowling alley were far above what Reggie had ever dreamed. And there was a whopping big budget for television and internet advertising.

Reggie sat down in the swivel chair and counted to ten. But his curiosity got the better of him and he turned to page three of the ledger, which revealed the new costs of running the expanded zoo.

He almost had a heart attack. The costs of running the new entertainment attractions were astronomical while the figures for running the zoo itself were miniscule.

Furthermore, the salary for one new veterinarian was well below the minimum salary for that need. How could the zoo find a vet who would work so cheaply? Moreover, one vet wouldn't be sufficient for all the new animals, would it? And where was the budget for assistants to help feed the zoo livestock and clean the cages of the new animals?

Then Reggie glanced at his own salary. "They expect me to work for that?" he exclaimed out loud. "They've cut my wages, even though I paid the zoo tax! This is outrageous!"

## Chapter Five

The unfamiliar sound of a motorcycle engine pierced the air at 8:00 in the morning, right outside Reggie's cottage. It sputtered, wheezed, and died—and then there was a loud knock at the door.

Reggie opened it and looked down upon a quite small person wearing a Taylor Swift T-shirt, blue jeans, motorcycle boots, a white helmet, and carrying a black canvas bag.

"Sorry to bother you, sir, but I'm looking for a Mr. Goodenough."

"You've found him," Reggie replied, "But please call me Reggie."

"Thanks, Reggie. President Flommock told me that you would show me the ropes. I'm new here."

"I've worked at this zoo for a number of years, but I can't recall seeing any ropes," Reggie joked. "We have some chains. Want to see them?"

"No thanks. 'Showing someone the ropes' is a figure of speech meaning to make them familiar with the operations of a place…in this case, the zoo."

"I was pulling your leg," Reggie laughed. "I am well-aware of that old navy expression first used by sailors instructing new recruits. But excuse me. Who are you?"

"I'm the new veterinarian. My name is Abby Sweet." She removed her helmet, freeing her medium long, brown hair to puff out from her helmet rather attractively. She held out her hand and Reggie shook it.

"Aha!" he exclaimed, surprised. "I see you are of the female persuasion. The motorcycle must have confused me. The only motorcycles around here belong to men who are members of the Senior Citizen's Harley Davidson Motorcycle Club. You had better come in and have some peppermint tea."

Abby Sweet sat on the comfortable sofa in the living room, and Reggie went into the kitchen to prepare the tea. He called to her. "How do you take it? I like mine with a little honey. Our bees collected it just last week."

"Honey would suit me just fine," Abby Sweet answered, "But I'm sorry to tell you that bees don't actually collect honey. They collect nectar from flowers, which turns into honey inside their bodies."

Reggie appeared at the kitchen door, wiping his hands on a dishcloth. "You are absolutely right!" he exclaimed. "Honey itself doesn't grow on flowers. If it did, we wouldn't need bees!"

They sipped their tea and Reggie insisted she eat some of his home-baked apple pie, which she found delicious. He noticed her eyelashes were the longest he had ever seen. Magnified by her thick glasses, they resembled large spiders.

"The glass in your spectacles seems rather thick," Reggie observed.

"Very true," Abby Sweet agreed. "Beside being of extremely short stature, I am also exceptionally near-sighted, quite myopic in fact."

"Good Gorillas!" Reggie exclaimed. "That must cause you some difficulty when you examine animals."

"I do okay, but I have to admit I haven't examined very many of them since I only graduated from Veterinary College last week."

Reggie suddenly understood why the directors placed such a small amount of money in the budget for the new vet's salary. In order to have more funds for their games and rides, they hired the least expensive recent graduate they could find.

"Well, you don't have anything to worry about here," Reggie said. "My animals are all pretty healthy and I'd be most pleased to give you a hand if any of them become ill."

"Are you a veterinarian, too?" Abby Sweet asked.

Reggie pondered the question. "Not quite. I am unskilled with medications, operations, pain locations, temperature variations, and emergency situations. However, much of the practice of animal medicine is just plain common sense. And we've never needed a full-time vet here at Lincoln Zoo. Once in a great while, I've called in Dr. McGillicuddy from the Bedside Manor Retirement Home. He helped cure a few maladies using people medicine."

"May I see the zoo now?" she asked.

"You bet! Follow me!"

Reggie gave Abby a tour of his garden, and she admired the profusion of flowers in bloom. In his greenhouse, he picked her a ripe bunch of succulent purple Concord grapes. She popped the yummy fruit into her mouth two-at-a-time as they made their way to the square and the new Veterinary Surgery building, which seemed to be better constructed than some of the other new buildings.

"Why, this is fantastic!" she exclaimed. Inside, the shelves were stocked with bottles and containers of medicines and every conceivable size of bandages, splints, and surgical tapes. And there were scales for weighing all sizes of animals. Another area contained dental instruments, drills, oxygen cylinders, and even laughing gas. A fully equipped operating room, complete with anesthetics and an X-ray machine, sat ready in case any animal became ill enough to need surgery.

"Where are the breeding rooms?" Abby Sweet asked.

Reggie looked pained. "Alas, there are none."

"But what about the baby animals? Where will I take care of them?"

"Unfortunately, you won't need to take care of them," Reggie replied. "We have always been a poor zoo and couldn't afford to buy mates. As a matter of fact, you could call this a '*postage stamp zoo.*' Many stamp collections only have one item from each country. It's the same here."

Abby Sweet was dismayed. "That is a crying shame."

"I agree," Reggie confessed, "But perhaps things will change when the new animals arrive from Africa. I hope the next step will be to persuade the Board of Directors that many of the animals should receive mates. Are you ready for your visit?"

"You bet!"

Reggie started out the door, but then stopped and looked around. "I wonder if you might have some vitamin injections handy. We've got a lethargic Lion, a traumatized Tiger, and a dog-tired old Wolf. I'd like to give them each a little shot to pep them up."

Abby Sweet looked inside one of the medicine cabinets. "Here's just the thing." She held up a large hypodermic needle and a bottle containing a multi-vitamin mixture. "I will bring them along."

Abby Sweet admired Reggie's environmental work at the Monkeys' cages. He had arranged authentic plants, flowers, shrubs, ferns, and trees from their own regions of Asia, Africa, and South America to make them feel more at home. He believed that a Spider Monkey swinging from a metal bar couldn't be as happy as one swinging from the branch of an acacia tree.

"Open the cages, please, Reggie, and I'll examine the Monkeys."

"Not necessary," Reggie pointed out. "These fellas are perfectly healthy. They're not suffering at all."

"How do you know?"

"Trust me, I just know," answered Reggie. "We have to check out Goliath now. He's having a bit of a Lion trauma. He's got the ego of a politician and an appetite to match. He usually eats nine pounds of ordinary meat a day, but now he won't even touch top grade-A sirloin. Would you like to give him the injection yourself?"

"Uh, sure." Abby Sweet took several deep breaths to steady herself. She didn't want to tell Reggie she had never given a shot to a Lion before. Reggie walked briskly towards the Lion's cage. Abby Sweet followed.

"What do you think of these cage decorations?" Reggie asked her, pointing out the canvas mural stretched across the back of the Lion House wall.

"Lovely," she said. But she wasn't really looking at the gorgeous sunset scene of the Serengeti National Park in Tanzania, East Africa that Reggie had painted himself. She was staring, transfixed, into the face of the Lion. Goliath's eyes squinted at her while he emitted a barely perceptible, low rumbling growl from the depths of his mighty chest. His tail, with its curious black tuft at the end, beat a slow menacing tattoo on the cement floor.

In spite of herself, Abby Sweet felt frightened. She tried to move but couldn't break her eyes from Goliath's squinty stare.

"I don't think you will be able to give him the injection from outside the cage, Abby Sweet," Reggie smiled, sensing her fear. He handed her a ring of keys. "Here are the keys. You enter the cage through the Lion House."

Abby froze for a moment, giving Reggie her best *'are you kidding me?'* Look.

"You'll be fine," Reggie comforted her.

The young vet took the keys and walked unsteadily into the cement structure.

Reggie quickly looked around to make sure none of the construction workers were watching him. Slowly, he put his hand through the bars and rested it on the Lion's head. Goliath opened his mouth and growled softly. In reply, Reggie cupped his hands around the Lion's ears and mumbled calm words. Then the giant Cat growled back. The old zookeeper barked at him sternly and Goliath stopped growling as he nodded in agreement.

Abby Sweet crawled through the narrow passage into the outer cage, trying to reassure herself, whispering under her breath, "You were an 'A' student, Abby Sweet. You can give a simple injection to a Lion."

She straightened up and checked her hypodermic needle, giving the plunger a little spurt to make sure it was working properly. She then stood, rooted to the spot, staring at Goliath through her thick glasses. The lion's tail stopped beating on the ground. His low growl had become a sort of purr.

Reggie called out, "Don't worry, Abby Sweet! He won't move an inch or make any threatening noises."

Abby Sweet closed her eyes and took a very deep breath. Her courage came to her in a wave. She walked confidently over to the Lion until she was close enough to smell his foul breath, thrust the needle into his hairy shoulder and pushed the plunger all the way in.

Goliath slowly raised his head and opened his gaping wide mouth.

"You p-p-promised he wouldn't move!" she cried, but she stood her ground. The Lion looked the young vet right in the face, winked his left eye, stuck out his tongue and licked her nose.

She gazed at him in amazement. Then she winked back and ruffled his golden mane with her small, delicate hands.

"I think you have just made your first animal friend at Lincoln Zoo," Reggie chuckled.

Abby Sweet grinned from ear to ear.

Luckily, Milt the Tiger was sound asleep. That morning, for the first time, the workmen had turned on the merry-go-round to test it. The big Cat was so dizzy from watching it go round and round that he slept soundly and didn't budge when Abby Sweet stuck the needle in his neck.

Reggie shook his head in dismay. "Tigers are supposed to be symbols of strength and energy," he told her. "Milt's a mess! His coat is getting dull and lifeless. I hope these injections work!"

"I'm pretty sure they will," Abby Sweet replied.

It was Leslie Wolf's turn next.

"Don't worry about Leslie. He's one of my oldest friends. Just give him this." Reggie handed her a rabbit-flavored treat bar. "He's got a very sweet tooth."

The young vet looked at Leslie's long, scary fangs as she warily entered his cage, the rabbit-flavored treat bar in her outstretched left hand and the syringe in her right. Leslie didn't even let her take a step inside. He leaped at her. She screamed. And in a flash, the Wolf had knocked her to the ground and went about munching one end of the treat bar.

With Leslie on top of her, she struggled to free her right arm from under him and finally was able to inject the vitamins into his chest.

"Let go of the treat bar, Abby Sweet," Reggie called out. She did, and Leslie bounded away to finish it, wrapper and all. She scrambled to her feet and slammed the cage door shut.

"This girl has guts," Reggie whispered to himself. Then he turned to Abby. "Leslie gets pretty excited about treats. Can't control himself. Sorry if he scared you."

"I think he surprised me more than scared me," she said, dusting herself off.

Leslie finished his snack, came over to the bars of the cage and barked sharply.

"He wants you to pet him," Reggie told her. Tentatively, Abby Sweet reached her hand out. The Wolf rubbed his head against her hand and then rolled over on his back for a belly rub!

"How peculiar," she thought. Wolves are not supposed to behave like this, except with people they have known for a long time. Maybe this Wolf thinks he's a Dog.

As they walked towards Reggie's cottage, Abby Sweet scratched her head. "This has been very strange!"

"Why is that?" Reggie asked.

"I have just made medical calls on animals I have never seen before, and they treated me with warmth, even affection. At vet school the animals were more aggressive and unfriendly."

"Well, perhaps you have developed a better cage-side manner," Reggie chuckled.

*Sounds fishy to me,* she thought to herself. "You're doing something to them, aren't you?"

"Who me? I don't know what you mean," Reggie answered, feigning innocence. "But I do fear that one injection does not a contented animal make in the miserable climate of this zoo."

At that moment, Throttlebottom waddled out of the office building and approached Reggie and Abby Sweet.

"You must be the new vet," he muttered, sticking out his limp hand, which Abby Sweet shook dutifully. "You look pretty small."

"Good things come in small packages," Reggie pointed out.

Throttlebottom yelled at him, "That's a great old saying, Pops. You'd better be right!" He pounded Reggie on the back.

"Gotta run, now," Throttlebottom sang. "I've got a hot deal cooking on a Canadian stock." And off he went, scurrying down the path towards his yellow stretch Cadillac parked in the brand-new parking lot.

As the zoo directors came out of the office building, Flommock spotted the zookeeper. "Reggie, I need to get over to my used car lot to do some business. So, when the new cages arrive, be sure to have the workmen put them in their correct positions around the zoo."

"You'll find the plan on my desk," Plitt said.

Winkleman turned to Plitt. "I got to hand it to you, Howard. You made one great deal on those cages. Seventy-five bucks each! What a fantastic businessman you are. No wonder your gas station is such a success."

"That may be true, Bill," admitted Plitt, "but your grocery store is doing terrifically well, and it's so clean."

"So is Big Max's Used Car Lot," Winkleman replied. "You could eat off the sink in the men's room!" Flommock beamed as the men continued to compliment each other and smile and pat one another on the back as they walked down the path to the parking lot.

## The Lincoln Zoo Rebellion

Later that afternoon, Reggie heard the insistent honking of an air horn by the entrance gates of the zoo. He hurried over to see what it was.

He found a giant transport truck parked on Lincoln Zoo Road with a sign painted on its side: 'Calhoun's Critter Cages.' The cargo bed was piled high with enormous gleaming metal cages. Reggie walked over to the driver's cab.

"Where shall I dump 'em, gramps?" Calhoun asked, not getting out of his truck. He was a lazy-looking man with a cigarette drooping from his mouth.

"Here is the plan." Reggie showed Calhoun the paper he had taken from Plitt's desk.

Calhoun took one look at the complicated drawing. "Hey, man, it ain't our job to place these cages around the zoo, man. Not for a lousy seventy-five bucks a pop, man!" He then pulled a hydraulic lever next to the hand brake, which tipped the back of the truck, causing the cages to slide off the platform and clatter loudly to the ground in a sprawling mass of metal.

Calhoun drove off, grinding gears down Belly Button Boulevard. "I guess it's true you get what you pay for," Reggie mumbled to himself. "You sure can't build a natural habitat for seventy-five spondulicks." Spondulicks was one of Reggie's favorite slang words for dollars along with "bucks," "simoleons," and "smackeroos".

The zookeeper persuaded some of the workmen building the video game arcade to place the cages according to the blueprint. They dragged each and all of them to their appointed positions around the zoo. The men were not gentle, and the cages clanged and clattered along the ground. Reggie thought they looked a bit too flimsy to hold active African animals.

## Chapter Six

Abby Sweet spent the rest of the afternoon settling into her new offices in the veterinary surgery building. She made lists of things to do and equipment to request. Every once in a while, she paused and scratched her head, wondering why it was so easy for her to give the animals their injections.

Several times, she gazed out the window and saw Reggie in the distance, hovering around the animals' cages. She found it curious that they seemed completely tame with him as they bleated, yelped, brayed, roared or barked.

The day passed quickly and, before she knew it, evening had arrived, and the construction workers had left for the day. The quiet of dusk had settled over the zoo. "I guess I'd better go to my lodgings too," she murmured to herself.

She turned off the lights and locked the front door of the surgery building. When she turned away from the door, she suddenly faced a surprise, and let out a startled little scream. There, staring her in the face, stood Goliath. Unimpressed by her reaction to him, he rotated on his heels and casually ambled away, his tail swishing in the wind.

Her heart beating quickly, she found herself following him. They walked past the square and the almost completed bowling alley and video game arcade. Occasionally, Goliath looked back to see if she was still there. They passed the pens of the Crocodile and Alligator, Adolf and Sigmund, and the cages of the Lynx, Cheetah, and Leslie Wolf.

She glanced at the Monkey cages. They were empty! She adjusted her glasses and looked again. They were still empty. Then she heard squealing and gleeful crying, and she witnessed a remarkable sight.

In the playground, beyond the cages, she saw Reggie. He was swinging back and forth in a child's swing being pushed by Durante, the Proboscis Monkey with an exceptionally large nose. The other Monkeys were gleefully cavorting on the bars and slides, while Milt the Tiger purred as he rolled around on his back.

"What in the world?" she exclaimed! Reggie heard her.

"I thought you had gone home a long time ago, Abby Sweet. Come on over here. Want to swing?"

"No, I don't want to swing. I would like an explanation, right this minute. You're letting dangerous beasts of the jungle roam around the zoo freely at night and they are behaving like tame little lambs. Do you have some sort of magic power over them?"

"There's nothing magical here," Reggie replied. "I can't even do a card trick. But I am going to need your help at this zoo, Abby Sweet. The animals will suffer because of these new games and rides and the only way I can think of helping them is for the two of us to work closely together. In order to do so, I must reveal to you a secret, but you must never tell a single soul."

"I promise." Abby Sweet sat down on the grass at Reggie's feet. Several Monkeys, including Louie the Lemur, imitated her action, and sat next to her. Durante stopped pushing Reggie's swing and Goliath plopped his five-hundred-pound bulk down to the ground and rested his head on his paws.

"Well, I guess it all started with a Canadian Red Fox named Hugh," Reggie began.

"Who's Hugh?" she asked, tingling with excitement.

Reggie continued. "One morning, shortly after I began working here, I came out of my cottage and there he sat, a Canadian Red Fox, resting on my doorstep. I showed him to a cage, and he trotted right in as if it were home.

"We got along famously. He was the first animal I would let out of his cage after the zoo closed to play hide-and-seek with his dinner. I used to do that with all the animals, by the way, until all the wooded areas were replaced by building developments."

Abby Sweet frowned. "You mean you used to let the animals forage for their food the way they do in the wild?" Reggie nodded. "You let them hunt?"

"Oh no, of course not," Reggie replied. "Most of these animals were born in captivity. They wouldn't know how to kill another animal. I just hid their meat in the woods so they would have to get exercise. Anyway, Hugh and I became the best of friends and, to make a long story shorter, he taught me to speak Fox."

"*Speak* Fox? Did I hear you right?"

"Perfectly, my dear. All animals make sounds and have motions and signs which, put together, *are* languages. Fox was the first one I learned many years ago."

Abby Sweet's mouth dropped open as Reggie continued.

"Hugh told me of his remarkable life. He was so caring and gentle he even made friends with other species. Why, he once saved three orphan Wolf cubs from certain death in a terrible storm by keeping them warm and fed. You've heard of humanitarians? Well, old Hugh was an *animalitarian*! I just made that up. Like it?"

"Love it," Abby Sweet cooed.

"Hugh became close with all the Canines we had here at the zoo and, because he knew some of their languages, he was able to help me learn them. We had a Dingo, Coyote, Jackal, and Wolf at that time.

"Over the years, Hugh and I had some great times together and some funny ones. I'll never forget the time that I smuggled him into a baseball game under my coat. He was fascinated! We were sitting in the stands, when a long ball was hit on the ground to the right fielder. Well, old Hugh couldn't contain himself. He jumped on to the field and stole the ball! The sight of all those men chasing a Fox on the field just broke me up."

"What happened?" Abby asked.

"Well, Hugh was so fast, he just disappeared. He turned up at the cottage later and told me he had played a practical joke. He got into the dressing room and hid the ball in the umpire's underpants! I could tell you stories about Hugh all night; he was such a great Fox. And a great friend.

"Anyway, some years later, I learned something quite remarkable, but under tragic circumstances. Late one night I heard Hugh barking that he wanted to talk to me urgently. I ran from my cottage and found him panting and feverish; his bark had turned to a hollow cough.

"He asked me to place my hand on his forehead, since he was losing his voice completely. As I did so, words and thoughts from Hugh's brain miraculously came into my own head. I realized he was communicating without speech! But it was not a thought I wished to hear. He told me his heart had been seized by a terrible pain and he felt he didn't have long to live.

"I closed my eyes and concentrated very hard. I prayed for my friend, telling the Almighty how much I loved this Fox and all he had taught me.

"Then, believe it or not, my head was bombarded with Hugh's brain waves again! He had heard my prayer! He understood every word! But it was too late. He thanked me for my love and appreciation, and he asked me to bury him next to the cottage. And then, with a little whimper, he died.

"The next morning, I dug a grave by the well near my cottage. I let all the Canines out of their cages, and we had a funeral for Hugh before the zoo opened. We were all so sad.

A glistening tear appeared behind Abby Sweet's thick glasses.

"But that morning I discovered I could communicate with the others without speech as well. It was easier if I placed my hands on their heads. We were surprised and pleased that we no longer had to bark or growl at each other all the time. We sure were going to miss old Hugh, but we were all thankful for his wonderful gift of communication.

"Now, don't get the wrong idea, Abby Sweet, I'm only truly fluent in Fox and Wolf. I do pretty well in most of the others, but I can't communicate with Dogs of the Asian countries. Come to think of it, I can't speak Japanese either."

"I can," Abby Sweet mumbled, quite in awe of what she was hearing. "I learned it at university."

"Oh, that's excellent!" Reggie continued. "Over the years, my powers of concentration got stronger and stronger. Sometimes I could close my eyes and communicate without touching the animals, even from afar.

"It took me quite a while to master the Feline or Cat tongues. Tiger and Cheetah came relatively quickly. Lion was a little tougher because of the guttural dialect, and I had to take singing lessons to expand my vocal range. Lynx and Jaguar were really tough. Lynx hurt my larynx and Jaguar made me hoarse for weeks. But eventually I learned. Projecting thoughts to the Big Cats with just my mind got easier and easier.

"Then, I took a long break away from the zoo. I traveled the world. I even crossed the Atlantic on a freighter and made a few Whale, Dolphin, and Porpoise friends on the way.

"When I returned, I plunged into my studies of Marsupial languages including Wallaby, Kangaroo, and Wombat. I studied

## The Lincoln Zoo Rebellion

Equus speech—Horse, Zebra, Donkey and their relatives. I had a Whale of a time, pardon the expression, with Antelope, Deer, Giraffe, Goat, and Hippo lingos.

"And then our poor little zoo got lucky. We received a number of Monkeys and Prosimians—which are primates—free of charge, from a zoo that had collapsed in bankruptcy! There were two Prosimians: a Ring-tailed Lemur and a Bush Baby. And a bunch of Monkeys, including a Brown Capuchin, a Golden Marmoset, a King Colobus and more. Learning to speak to them was easier than finding an ice cube in Siberia! One second, Abby Sweet. Let me just translate that for our friends here."

Reggie squealed and chattered for a few moments and meowed at Louie the Lemur. The Monkeys cackled and laughed at his Siberia joke even though they had no clue where or what Siberia was.

Reggie continued in English for Abby Sweet. "On my next vacation, I visited many excellent zoos around America that had species ours couldn't afford. I discovered I could speak with most of the other Primates including Gorillas, Chimpanzees, Baboons, and Orangutans. I had no trouble with Bear either.

"And I guess that's about it. I can't speak any Reptile, Bird, Fish, or Amphibian jargon, except for a few basic commands in Ostrich, Crocodile, and Alligator.

"Today, as we visited the animals, I whispered to them when you weren't looking and projected mind images to them. I made them promise not to be difficult and to take their treatment bravely. They gave me their assurances before I gave you the keys to their cages. So, there it is: my secret."

Abby Sweet sat, staring at Reggie for a few moments, astonished at what she had just heard. "May I ask a few questions?"

Before Reggie could answer, Durante, the Proboscis Monkey, who had been looking up into the sky, leaned over and chattered in Reggie's ear.

"I think that's enough for tonight, Doctor Abby Sweet," Reggie replied. "The animals are telling me a storm is about to sneak up on us and it's only a few minutes away."

Right on cue, the sound of distant thunder exploded, and the breeze turned suddenly colder in the night.

"Don't worry, Reggie. I won't tell a soul," Abby Sweet whispered.

Reggie smiled.

"You were reading my mind-projection, my dear, sweet lady. That's good."

## Chapter Seven

The e-mail the zoo directors were expecting finally arrived. Throttlebottom read it out to zoo directors gathered in the conference room. He cleared his throat:

Larry Belling with Art Twain

*From Jobiconn@cagr.ga*

*Assortment of Snakes and Lizards, Aardvark, Chimpanzee named Fingers, Hyena and Ostrich missed airplane. We have a good chance of getting you a rare female Eastern Lowland Gorilla and Baboon if you can wait. Also, we are hoping to send a Leopard, Wildebeest, Gazelle, and Black Rhino. Will send entire order together by ship when animals are collected. Sorry if this is any inconvenience to you, old bean.*
*Yours truly, Jobi Conn O'Brien.*

"I guess we have to face it, men," Throttlebottom declared. "We may not have new animals for the grand re-opening, but we *will* have the most entertaining new zoo in the country. Now, the first order of business at this meeting is our zookeeper."

"Reggie?" Winkleman and Flommock asked in unison. They were surprised.

"Yes. Reggie Goodenough. *THAT* old zookeeper. I am sure he is far too old to be the keeper of our new, improved zoo."

"How old is he?" Winkleman inquired.

"He never told me directly. But I've looked at the zoo's records and he's been with the zoo long enough for me to consider him to be much too old for our new zoo plans."

"So you *don't* know his age?" Flommock asked.

Throttlebottom paused and cast a hard look at Flommock. Through clenched teeth he hissed, "I don't need to know. Just look at him."

"I have looked at him," Flommock spoke up meekly. "To me, Reggie doesn't look a day over sixty, Ralph! His skin is smoother than mine, for goodness' sake!"

"So, what should we do about it?" the mayor asked.

"I say *fire* the old coot," Plitt replied. "He's an arrogant old pain-in-the-bottom anyway. Let's find someone younger."

Flommock agreed. "We'll kick the old geezer out, and then we can use his cottage as a toy museum." Throttlebottom perked up.

"Great idea!"

"Hang on a second," cautioned Winkleman. "We must consider the public reaction to eliminating the old Dog. Don't forget he's loved by everyone in Lincoln. We don't want to take any chances that people might not approve of our action and decide not to come to our glorious new zoo."

"That argument is complete balderdash!" Throttlebottom insisted. "People will come whether or not the old Dodo is here. But just to be safe, we won't tell anybody we're firing him. This is classified. All lips are sealed. All in favor?"

Everyone voted "Aye."

"This top-secret motion is passed," the mayor proclaimed. "Flommock! Give Reggie a pink slip tomorrow after the opening celebrations—and make sure he's out of that cottage in a week. And be sure to call the employment agency and order a new young zookeeper who will work cheap and be willing to live in Lincoln. Be sure to specify a 'male.' I don't trust women, but don't you dare tell anybody that."

## Chapter Eight

Meanwhile, eight thousand miles away at the Central African Mbinguni Game Reserve, Peter Nelson N'gara came bounding into Jobi Conn's breakfast room just as Jobi was finishing his breakfast.

"Jobi Conn!" Peter said with excitement. "Come outside and look at this Okapi. I've never seen one before. It's a beauty!"

The Okapi is a truly rare animal with Zebra-striped legs, the body of a Donkey, and the face of a Giraffe, but with a normal length of neck. It's a Giraffe's only relative. Jobi Conn walked all around the animal, which had been brought into camp that morning by three Pygmies—all under five feet tall—from a rescue wildlife reserve in the Ituri rainforest of the Congo. He ran his hands up and down the black-and-white striped legs of the Okapi and peered into its mouth.

"This may be the handsomest Okapi in all of Africa, Joe!" Jobi Conn shouted to Joe Otoronga. "Pay these little fellows a fair price in silver and tell them to stick around for lunch." Jobi Conn always paid the Pygmies in silver since paper money was of no use to them in the rain forest.

The gathering of animals for the Lincoln Zoo had just taken a turn for the better. Jobi Conn had tried to please Mayor Throttlebottom by sending the animals he had already collected by air. But unfortunately, a sudden rainstorm had flooded the region and his trucks could not get to the airport in time.

When the storm lifted, tribesmen from different wildlife rescue reserves began arriving in camp every day with new animals for Jobi Conn to consider buying. The various tribes worked with wildlife rescue reserves across Africa to help save and care for needy wildlife. Most animals on the mayor's list were first located by exchanging e-mails with rescue reserves, but Jobi Conn would not buy any animal he didn't personally check out. So, they were brought to the Mbinguni Rescue Reserve by working tribesmen from various reserves. Jobi Conn rejected some of the animals as being too old or not in perfect health, but others he bought gladly. Some Kikuyu tribesmen brought a robust female Leopard. Another tribe presented a healthy Wildebeest, also known as a Gnu, and a Thompson's Gazelle. But, best of all, Maasai tribesmen arrived with a particularly large, extremely rare Black Rhino with one of the longest front horns any of them had ever seen. The animal had been found, with a foot caught in a poacher's trap, and after several months of care, its injured leg healed nicely. But the animal was slowed down by the injury and would have been at risk if attacked by predators in the wild.

Also, good news had arrived from Senegal in West Africa, where a colleague of Jobi Conn's had rehabilitated a magnificent specimen: a full-grown female Eastern Lowland Gorilla! Arrangements had been made to transport her to Jobi Conn's camp.

Surprisingly, no one had been able to find any Baboons, although they're usually very plentiful, and drew a blank on Elephants, which had become scarce due to illegal poaching. "If worse comes to worst, we may have to send Blomm," Joe Otoronga suggested.

Peter shuddered at the thought of placing that stubborn, unfriendly African Elephant in a peaceful American zoo, and the havoc he might cause if anyone came near him with a long wooden stick.

The local postman shared the ominous news that the secret police still had an all-points bulletin out for Peter. They were even offering a reward.

There had been a major panic when a group of strangers arrived in camp. Peter was rushed to Jobi Conn's secret hiding place, but it was a false alarm. It turned out that the men were not secret police, but only hunters seeking Black Rhino for their horns. When Jobi Conn heard that, he went ballistic!

"You must never set foot in this region again, you villainous miscreants!" he snapped. "You would kill Black Rhinos for their horns! Shame on you! You are lucky I don't have time to call the police on you!" He fired his rifle into the air and the men ran off, properly frightened.

Available space on transport ships to America from the port of Mombasa was hard to come by, but Jobi Conn had some friends in the shipping office of an East Indian line, and he knew the captains of several of the ships. He received an e-mail saying that one of their ships, the Hornbill, could transport his shipment of animals in twenty days, but they could not promise another vessel for three months.

This threw Jobi Conn into a tizzy. "We must leave for Mombasa tomorrow!" he growled. "Get the trucks ready. Load the cages. We'll have to send Blomm. And we'll have to find a Baboon later. Hurry! We don't have a moment to spare!"

Joe Otoronga was thrilled. "You know that next week will be the annual harvest festival in the port of Mombasa. After we deliver the animals to the ship, we can all dress up and join the parade."

Every autumn, residents of the port town would don costumes of giant fruit and vegetables and march through the town, celebrating the harvest. There would be musical bands riding on large floats covered with flowers. Joe made sure his usual costume of a huge carrot hadn't been eaten by moths as he gathered a number of other costumes for the men.

Jobi Conn's orders were obeyed immediately, creating a flurry of activity around the camp. Peter helped the native workers—Kafi, Evaristo, Mitch, and a strong, seven-foot-tall giant named Curly—get the animals ready for the five-day journey to Mombasa. The cages containing the Okapi, Leopard, Aardvark, Chimpanzee, Wildebeest, Gazelle, Black Rhino, Blomm (the Elephant) and other animals were loaded onto the trucks in preparation for an early morning departure.

That evening everyone sat down to a huge feast celebrating a job well done. The menu included Antelope steak, spaghetti with Ostrich meatballs, and a slimy side-dish made from lizards that Peter avoided. After dinner, Peter helped Jobi Conn pack his suitcase for the journey ahead. "May I please come with you?" Peter implored. "I've heard so much about the port of Mombasa, but I have never seen it."

"Sorry old bean," cautioned Jobi Conn. "With those bloody secret policemen looking for you, it would be far too dangerous!"

The next morning, Peter was awakened by groans from the next tent that sounded like a chorus made up of Kafi's high-pitched whines, Evaristo's melodic groans, and throaty moans that could only be Mitch's. He rushed into the tent to discover the three men writhing on the floor.

"What's wrong?" Peter cried.

"It must be something we ate last night," moaned Mitch. "My stomach is turning inside out! Curly didn't eat the slithering Lizard pâté and he seems to be okay."

"I didn't have it either and I am fine," replied Peter. "So are Joe and Jobi Conn. They're okay, too."

It was decided that the three moaning men were too ill to travel to Mombasa and that Peter would have to join Jobi Conn, Joe, and the giant, Curly, to help transport the animals.

"We must leave immediately," exclaimed Jobi Conn. "But we'd better use a disguise for Master Peter here." Joe held up his bag containing the fruit and vegetable costumes for the harvest festival parade. He handed it to Peter. "There should be something in here you can wear. Hold onto this for me."

Peter was delighted to be included in the journey to Mombasa, even if it meant wearing a silly-looking vegetable costume.

"Off we go!" cried Jobi Conn, and the caravan of three trucks driven by himself, Joe Otoronga, and the giant, Curly, revved up and lumbered down the dirt road and onto the highway to Mombasa. Peter sat up front, beside Jobi Conn.

Along the way they stopped at a watering hole for refreshment when, surprisingly, a Baboon jumped through the window of Jobi Conn's truck and refused to leave. While this was typical of Baboon behavior, it was also an amazing gift.

"It's a miracle!" Peter cried out.

"A stroke of good luck, old bean!" Jobi Conn agreed. "In our rush, I almost forgot we needed one of these chappies!" The ride to Mombasa suddenly became nicely relaxed.

In the bustling port city of Mombasa, Peter peered through the window of the moving truck. He was fascinated by the East Indian traders on the streets, pushing carts filled with colorful clothes and food delicacies. They passed some of the floats going through their final preparation for the harvest parade, busily being decorated with an abundance of the most beautiful flowers Peter had ever seen.

They drove straight to the port, where Peter marveled at the large number of fishing boats and dozens of people haggling over the prices of freshly caught fish. They quickly found the ship hired to transport the animals: the Hornbill.

Jobi Conn gave the files of paperwork required by the government for animals to be taken out of Africa to Joe Otoronga and Joe headed for the customs building on the dock to complete the details of the shipment.

"You stay in the truck and keep out of sight," Jobi Conn warned Peter. I'm going to visit my friend, the captain."

Jobi Conn walked up the gangplank and onto the deck, where he greeted the deck hands by name, as he knew them well from previous transactions and he was taken to the captain's office. Peter stayed in the cab of the truck. He looked out the rear window and found himself staring face to face, eyes locked, with the Elephant Blomm. Peter noticed a greenish liquid dripping from his eyes. He was snorting and breathing rapidly. One of the workmen noticed the same thing.

"It's the musth," the man cried out. "Someone should inform Joe Otoronga. It is very urgent." When Elephants get into a state called "musth," they become very aggressive indeed. This phenomenon usually happens once a year to Elephants, Camels, and a few other species and makes them extremely unpredictable, and dangerous.

"I'll go find Joe," Peter replied, jumping out of the truck.

Inside the grey building, he entered a long dark corridor with many closed doors. Peter could hear mumbling voices, but there was no telling where, in which office, Joe was dealing with the paperwork. Peter gently opened one of the doors but there was no one inside.

Then he heard the sound of marching men coming around the corner. He pressed his body against a wall, trying to be invisible. It must have worked. The men didn't seem to notice him as they opened one of the doors and marched into a room, leaving the door open.

Peter peeked through the doorway and saw his dear second cousin, Joe, being questioned by the police. "Joseph Otoronga!" one of the policemen said loudly. "I hope you are not guilty of hiding an enemy of our country, your second cousin: Peter Nelson N'gara. Now, if you know what's good for you, you will tell us where we can find that boy right now!"

"I'm sorry, but I cannot tell you," Joe lied. "I do not know where this boy is. I am trying to find him myself."

"I believe…" the Captain of Police paused for dramatic effect, "…that you are lying! We are going to lock you up until you tell the truth!" The captain barked an order and motioned three of the men to escort Joe out of the room in handcuffs.

Peter's legs turned to jelly. He braced himself against the wall in the corridor, his heart thumping like a jungle drum. He closed his eyes and wished he could just disappear into the floorboards.

"We know this boy is here in Mombasa somewhere," shouted the captain. "We have our sources! Let's go find him and arrest him and throw him into jail with his parents. March!" The rest of the policemen marched out of the building, walking in military step, chanting "Hup two three four…"

Peter was greatly relieved to hear his parents were still alive, although they were imprisoned. But he knew he could neither stay in Mombasa, nor go back to the Central African Mbinguni Game Reserve to hide out with Jobi Conn, since that would be the first place the police would search. But where could he go? Where could he be safe?

He took a few deep breaths and said to himself calmly, "I will figure this out, or my name is not Peter Nelson N'gara."

## Chapter Nine

Shortly before nine in the morning on the Saturday of the grand reopening celebration for the new Lincoln Zoo (even though the new animals had not yet arrived), Reggie walked down the main square, the keys to the iron gates jangling in his hands. He passed the new fifteen-foot statue of Ralph Bear that had been erected over a fountain dead center in the square. A stream of water squirted out of the Bear's mouth, reminding Reggie of Throttlebottom spitting out his mouthwash. The mayor had created the Ralph Bear stuffed doll at the toy factory long ago and shamelessly gave it his own first name, as though it was his own child. Now, the likeness of Ralph Bear was turned into a huge fountain statue, a monument to the mayor's ego.

Reggie walked down to the gates where the zoo's new employees had gathered, waiting to come in and start their first day of work. Most of them were college students, who he recognized as children who used to visit him after school. They called out "Good morning, Reggie!" and he welcomed them, trying his best to appear cheerful.

The new employees were dressed festively in multicolored hats and red shirts with 'LINCOLN ZOO' printed in bold white letters. In smaller white, shiny letters on the back of the shirts he could make out "Don't Miss the Toy Store."

Reggie inserted the new iron key in the padlock. It wouldn't turn. He laughed, thinking how ironic it would be if he couldn't open the gates and the whole grand reopening celebration had to be canceled.

He pulled out the key, found a hammer and metal file in his toolbox, and placed the key on a rock. He pounded it a few times, filed the edges, and tried again. The padlock opened in a flash. The new employees applauded, so Reggie hammed it up and took a little bow. The group ran up the pathway as he re-locked the gates to discourage any early customers.

The merry-go-round operators turned on the carousel's mechanism and it sprang to life with lights and bells and calliope music playing "Teddy Bears' Picnic." Reggie frowned at the noise, which was louder than he ever imagined it would be and especially because that particular tune seemed out of place, to say the least.

The video game arcade employees tested their loud-speaker equipment. "Step right up, ladies and gents," came blasting over the loudspeakers. Reggie had been surprised to discover the great variety of video games on offer and dismayed to see how violent they were. Many of them featured warlike situations, sword-fighting aliens, vicious monsters, and dangerous criminals. On one of them, players could shoot wild animals in Africa, which angered Reggie terribly. He was also dismayed that some of the shooting gallery targets were also cartoon animals.

Suddenly, a great wave of clanging machinery resounded like an earthquake. The clatter came from the bowling alley. Reggie ran to see what had happened. "Don't worry," the operator laughed. "That's the normal sound automatic pinsetters make when they start up."

Unhappy with the noise, Reggie sat down on a park bench and, holding his head, listened to the horrible sounds all around him. He tried to mind talk to the animals, suggesting they just ignore the noise—but it was hopeless.

Just before 10:00 a.m., Throttlebottom and his three henchmen, Flommock, Winkleman, and Plitt came out of their offices, dressed in their best business suits.

"Ah, there you are Reggie," bellowed Throttlebottom. "It's time for us to open the gates to our glorious new zoo. You got your keys?" Reggie nodded yes and held them up for the mayor to see. "Great. Follow us."

Reggie joined the four of them on their walk to the gates. On the way, Plitt slipped an envelope into Reggie's hand. "Put this in your pocket and open it later, Pops."

"What is it?" Reggie asked.

"You'll see," Plitt replied with a sardonic grin on his face, and Reggie stuffed the envelope into the pocket of his khakis.

At the gates, Reggie looked in amazement at the huge throng of people. It seemed as if the entire town had turned out and the local police force, headed by Chief Grant Buxton, held back the excited crowd. He saw Sadie standing there, clutching her ever-present bag of dried apricots, and Tiny Teeny waving while smiling her toothy smile, along with residents of the Bedside Manor Retirement Home, and Jovino Matzos and members of his Senior Citizens Harley Davidson Motorcycle Club (without their bikes)—all anxiously waiting to enter.

The Devilish Duo and other children, including Cory Chang, Jaime Gutierrez, LaToya Tricklebank, Melly Belloso, and Scooter Goldfarb filled out the crowd, along with the entire Scout Troop, carrying their swimming gear and eager to see the new pool. He recognized merchants from town who had closed their businesses for the day to join the celebration. He waved a greeting to Bernie Moon, the newspaper reporter for the *Lincoln Examiner* and sometimes television newsman, carrying his trusty camera.

A thick, gold-colored satin ribbon had been draped across the gates awaiting the right moment for Throttlebottom to snip with a pair of gigantic ceremonial scissors, and symbolically open the day.

"Okay, old man!" he called to Reggie at the top of his lungs. "Open 'em up!"

## The Lincoln Zoo Rebellion

Reggie unlocked the padlock, and as Bernie Moon furiously snapped pictures, Throttlebottom cut the ribbon and announced, "I hereby proclaim the new improved triple-size Lincoln Zoo open. Today, all the new attractions and games are free. And furthermore, anyone spending more than five dollars in the toy store gets a free Ralph Bear key chain."

Everyone cheered and rushed through the gates.

Just then, cymbals crashed, and the Lincoln High School Marching Band burst into the 1812 Overture as they began strutting up the path. The bass drum boomed and out-of-tune trumpets blared. Reggie clapped his hands to his ears and ran up to the band leader as he tossed a silver baton into the air.

"This is going to scare the animals!" Reggie shouted. But the loud music drowned him out, and the Drum Major was concentrating too hard on catching his baton.

"I give up!" Reggie cried, running towards his cottage. He ducked inside and slammed the door shut. He closed the windows to help shut out as much noise as possible and removed his shoes and khakis. The envelope dropped out of the pocket onto the floor.

He picked it up and sliced it open with his fingernail. The words on the pink piece of paper were a blur. He wiped his eyes and tried to focus. Then he read the paper over and over again, not believing it could be true. But it was. The paper read:

*From: the Board of Directors, Lincoln Zoo*

*To: Mr. R. Goodenough.*

*Thank you for your service to the Lincoln Zoo. We are pleased to let you know that you have now been retired because of your extremely old age. We would appreciate you leaving your cottage within two weeks as we wish to turn it into a toy museum.*

*Yours faithfully, Lincoln Zoo directors.*

"I haven't retired!" Reggie exclaimed aloud. "I have been fired! This has been my home for as long as I can remember. How can they do this to me?" He thought for a moment, then shook his head. "I think I will have to take a nap!"

The old zookeeper put on a pair of emerald green pajamas and his woolly bedroom slippers and climbed the creaking wooden steps to his sleeping platform. He rolled into his bed.

A half hour later he awoke with a start. *How disappointing not to have a dream. A nap without a dream is like tea without honey*, he thought to himself. He opened the window in his roof, stood on top of his bed, looked out over the zoo and observed the throngs of people enjoying themselves.

The Scouts cavorted around the swimming pool, supervised by their handsome scoutmaster. People were bowling, swimming, playing video games, and happily riding the merry-go-round. The school band paraded around the zoo, playing music out of tune. As far as he could see, the only two people in the entire zoo looking at an animal were Sadie and Tiny Teeny, sitting on a bench in front of Sam the Giraffe's cage, munching dried apricots and cotton candy. Reggie shook his head, sadly.

Bernie Moon spotted Reggie poking his head through the window in his roof. The reporter especially noticed Reggie's emerald green pajamas.

"How strange," Moon mumbled out loud to himself. "What logical reason could there be for Reggie to be in bed in the middle of this day of all days?" His eyebrows wrinkled in thought.

"Aha!" he cried, jumping to a conclusion. "He must be ill." *On the other hand*, he thought, *Reggie has never been sick a day in his life. And on the third hand, there is always a first time.*" Bernie Moon took out his trusty notebook and scribbled an entry:

*Reggie sick? Why not joining celebration?*

Moon wandered down to the main square and took a few photographs of Ralph Bear spewing water into the fountain. He felt a bit dejected since the grand reopening of the zoo was going too smoothly and he was hoping for something out of the ordinary to happen so he could get himself on the six o'clock TV news and make an additional $25.00.

Often, quotations from officials can spice up an otherwise dull article, so Moon was pleased when he spotted Big Max Flommock and Howard Plitt walking towards the flimsy office building. "Oh good! I can kill two Birds with one stone."

"How's it going, gentlemen?" Moon asked.

"Splendid," Plitt answered.

"Very good, Moon," Flommock added.

"Have there been any problems at all?"

"Nope." Plitt said. "Everything is hunky dory."

"Surely *not everybody* is one hundred percent happy," Moon probed.

"Wrong, Moon!" Flommock retorted. "If you're looking for dirt, Moon, you're not going to find it here. You'd be better off asking the Man in the Moon, Moon." Flommock giggled uncontrollably at his own witticism.

"Then, why do you think your zookeeper, Reggie Goodenough, has taken to his bed?"

"Well, Moon, you see, it's like this, Moon. The old geezer…" Flommock began.

Plitt abruptly grabbed Flommock by the arm. "Sorry, Moon. We've got an urgent meeting. Good luck with your story and thanks for writing that the new improved zoo is fabulous."

Plitt dragged Flommock into the office building to prevent him from revealing they were removing Reggie from his job. Sensing some interesting news, Moon followed them over to the office building and snuck around to the back. He spotted Throttlebottom sitting at a desk, sipping coffee. He gently slid up the window a bit so he could hear.

Plitt pushed Flommock into Throttlebottom's office. "Sorry to interrupt, boss, but Max here almost told that fake newsman about Reggie."

"I am extremely disappointed in you, Max," snapped Throttlebottom. "You could have caused a public relations disaster!"

"I'm sorry, Ralph," Flommock apologized. "I didn't mean to do anything wrong."

"Well, never let it happen again. You must leave all the important announcements to me!"

"Okay Ralph," Flommock promised. "I won't tell anyone that we are firing Reggie and turning his cottage into a toy museum."

Bernie Moon's mouth sprung open, wide in surprise. He slammed the window shut and took off. Plitt and Flommock ran to the window to see what the slamming noise was about and saw the reporter scurrying briskly down the path.

"It's Moon. He heard us, Ralph!" exclaimed Flommock.

"Tarnation and darn it!" the mayor groaned, using stronger unprintable words.

Bernie Moon slowed down as he passed the Veterinary Surgery building. At that moment Abby Sweet came rushing out of the door and ran right into him. He caught her before she could fall.

"I'm terribly sorry, but I didn't see you coming." Bernie apologized. "I'm Bernie Moon of the *Lincoln Examiner*...and sometimes on TV. Who are you?"

"I'm Abby Sweet, the new vet, and I'm just going out to check on some animals." She adjusted her thick glasses and started blinking and rubbing her eye. "I think I've got something in my eye."

"Let me look." Moon reached his hand to her face. "Aha! Let me just remove this piece of thread."

"Ouch!" she cried. "That's no thread, you ninny. It's my eyelash!"

"Oh, I'm terribly sorry," Moon apologized. "You sure have some whopping great eyelashes. They look like spiders!"

"That's not terribly flattering." Abby Sweet made a sour face.

"No, no! What I mean is they're really lush and frame your eyes with beauty and sophistication," purred Moon.

"That's a little better," Abby Sweet admitted, softened by the sweet words. "So, what are you going to write about this so-called amusing new zoo with no new animals?"

"I just got myself a real scoop," Moon gushed. "It appears that the Board of Directors is going to fire the old zookeeper."

"Reggie? Oh my, no! That's terrible news! I've only known him for a few weeks, but I'm mad about him! I really need this job, but I don't want to work for people who would do such a cruel and heartless thing."

"Everybody loves him," agreed Moon. "I've known him since I was a boy. He used to feed us berries and melons after school.

He always treated us like his own children. He's the best. I've got to help him! Come with me."

Bernie Moon and Abby Sweet walked together to Reggie's cottage.

Reggie appeared at the kitchen door; with a pink piece of paper stuffed in the pocket of his green pajama top. "Do you want a snickerdoodle, Bernie? I remember giving you one for the first time twenty years ago when you were seven."

"Forget your butter and cinnamon cookies, Reggie!" Moon said. "I just heard the news."

"News?" Reggie hoped it wasn't the news of his firing.

"They can't fire you, Reggie. You're an institution, the longest serving public person in all of Lincoln. I'll write articles in the paper. I'll put you on my TV show. After the public outcry, you will certainly be reinstated!"

"Relax, my boy. Perhaps it's for the best. Maybe the public feels a younger man or woman could do a better job."

"But where would you go? Do you have any family?"

"No, I have never been blessed with a family of my own, but I'm pretty sure they'll give me a bed at the Bedside Manor Retirement Home. At least I could ride my bicycle here and visit my animals. I don't want to leave, but..."

"No buts!" cried Moon, a look of hard determination on his face. "I want action. I want...the front page!" He plucked the pink paper from the pocket of Reggie's pajamas, stormed out of the cottage, and walked briskly back to the office building, leaving Amy Sweet still standing with Reggie. Moon knocked loudly on the door to Throttlebottom's office.

"Come in," Throttlebottom sang, and Moon entered. "We were expecting you after your low-down spying on us."

Moon ignored the insult. "Are you willing to give me some answers on the record?" he began.

"Okay, this is now an official press conference," declared the mayor. "As you already know, we've decided to retire Reggie the zookeeper."

Moon's eyebrows hit the top of his forehead. "Retire?"

"That's right, Moon. *Retire*, as in honorably remove him from service because of extreme old age. He's leaving. That's it, that's all, the press conference is over so goodbye and good luck!"

"I don't think so," Moon sneered. "First of all, you didn't retire him, you fired him, and I've got the pink slip to prove it." He waved the pink paper in the air. "Now, I don't want to write a story about unfair zoo bosses taking away an old man's home and livelihood. I would prefer to write a story about a mayor's wisdom and the Board of Directors' generosity.

"'Wisdom and generosity' do sound a lot nicer, Ralph," Winkleman agreed.

"What's the catch?" Throttlebottom snapped.

"Well, I think it would be much nicer if you allow Reggie to stay in the cottage as long as he lives. You should give him a generous pension, and the title 'Honorary Zookeeper for Life,' and an assistant to do some of the heavier work."

"That's ridiculous!" Plitt complained. "That cottage is on valuable property. He can't stay there forever."

"You're very greedy, Moon," hissed Throttlebottom.

Bernie Moon looked at his watch. "I'm waiting. My newspaper deadline is in seventeen minutes."

The zoo directors mumbled and whispered together for a few minutes.

"Okay, Moon," Throttlebottom grumbled. "I guess you've got us against the wall. We will allow Reggie to stay in the cottage and we will pay him half his salary for sitting around doing nothing. You can write your story so long as you include the words 'wisdom' and 'generosity.' Deal?"

"Deal," they all declared together, and Bernie Moon tore the pink piece of paper in half.

The mayor pointed his finger at the reporter. "This heralds a new era for the zoo. Write that down, Moon. And don't forget to put my picture on the front page!"

The mayor looked forward to a glowing article in the next day's Lincoln *Examiner* about his humanity and kindness. He rather needed it since there was considerable unrest among the workers at his toy factory. Many of them were coming down with mysterious illnesses requiring medical attention or staying at home without explanation.

"Now, they will have to call me 'Mister Good Guy.'"

Early the next morning, Throttlebottom waited impatiently on the front porch of his fake castle for the newsboy to deliver the *Examiner*. He waddled across the drawbridge that sat over the moat to make sure he caught the boy before he tossed the newspaper into the water for the third time that week.

Inside the castle, he ripped open the paper and stared at the front page. A large photograph of Reggie and Abby Sweet stared back at him. "Where's my picture?" he yelled out loud. Then he read the headline and turned purple with rage.

### REPORTER THWARTS THREAT
### TO FIRE ZOOKEEPER
by Bernard Moon

## The Lincoln Zoo Rebellion

Due to the efforts of this reporter, threats by Mayor Throttlebottom and the Board of Directors of Lincoln Zoo to fire zookeeper Reggie Goodenough were reversed yesterday.

They were about to fire the lovable public servant and throw him out of his lifelong home on the grounds of the zoo when this reporter caught wind of the situation and stepped in to negotiate on the zookeeper's behalf.

As a result, the directors saw the *wisdom* of a better way and, with reluctant *generosity*, they agreed to let him stay, pay him a modest pension, and give him the title 'Honorary Zookeeper for Life.'

Although he is now retired, Reggie confirmed that he plans to continue his duties with the help of the zoo's new veterinarian, long-lashed Abigail Sweet. The Board has also agreed to hire him an assistant in the near future, hopefully before the new animals arrive from Africa.

Mayor Ralph Throttlebottom, who also heads the local toy factory, which has had its share of trouble lately from workers bitter about low pay as well as suffering from mysterious diseases, heralded a new era for the zoo.

Throttlebottom started to hiccough and couldn't stop. "I'll have-*HIC*-that hack's job-*HIC*-if I have to buy the whole hicking *Examiner*!" he sputtered. He threw the newspaper out the window into the moat.

## Chapter Ten

Letters flooded into the newspaper from all over Lincoln and surrounding areas in such volume that postman Zack Wineapple nearly sprained his back trying to lift the heavy mail sacks. Most of the letters expressed outrage that the Board of Directors of the zoo had even considered firing Reggie; some of them were published by the *Examiner's* editor.

## LETTERS TO THE EDITOR

*Those dirty Ratfinks. I cannot sign my name to this letter because I work as a Wombat stuffer at the toy factory, and I don't want you-know-who to do to me what he tried to do to poor old Reggie.*
*Anonymous*

*How dare they even think about firing Reggie? Who voted for those creeps anyway? I bet you don't have the guts to publish this letter. Well, you better. I pay my taxes. I even paid the zoo tax. That's right, I am mad. If you don't publish this letter, I'm going to get really really mad.*
*Casper B. Ryetoast*

*I have just added up the ages of the zoo directors and realized they are 219 years old. Let's fire them!*
*Buffy Uffner*

*If more elderly people like Reggie could keep their jobs, we wouldn't need crummy old people's homes. Also, we hate being called Senior Citizens, so stop it this minute!*
*Tiny Teeny and Sadie*

*When I was a boy, Reggie taught me everything about edible plants. Now I am doing important scientific work in gene splicing of vegetables. In fact, yesterday I crossed a pumpkin with a potato. They'll be so huge I'll put little engines on them and sail them across the oceans to feed hungry people in Africa. I am going to call it them 'potumkins.'*
*Albert J. Broccoli*

## The Lincoln Zoo Rebellion

*Reggie taught me to recognize different kinds of trees. I'll bet his bosses don't know their ash from an elderberry.*
*Jaimie Gutierrez Age 11*

But two days later, the letters ceased and many of the people who had written in hoping to see their comments printed in the newspaper wondered why letters of complaint stopped appearing in the paper. Then, on Saturday, a small article appeared at the bottom of the financial page:

### EXAMINER SOLD TO SYNDICATE

The *Examiner* has been sold to a syndicate of investors from Canada headed by investment banker, Harold G. Koonin. A number of editorial staff changes will include the appointment of a new editor. Reporter Bernard Moon has been moved to the gardening page.

Most people, however, didn't even notice the small article because they were too excited about the big news on the front page. The new animals were on their way from Africa! Much of the front page was taken up with a photograph of Mayor Throttlebottom smiling radiantly and holding up an e-mail printout.

From: Jobiconn@cagr.ga

Good news, Mayor Throttlebottom. The wait is over! Complete animal order has been collected and shipped on East Indian vessel, *Hornbill*, docking New York harbor in twenty weeks from Wednesday. Train will arrive at Lincoln on that Friday at 3:49 p.m. Animals all healthy, but be extremely careful with the Elephant called Blomm, who might have the musth.

Yours truthfully, Jobi Conn O'Brien.

"Is everything ready?" Abby Sweet asked Reggie. She was hurriedly packing various medical instruments into her traveling medical bag.

"I think so. I seem to have laid in enough food for half the animal population of Nigeria," he exaggerated.

The two of them rode into town together on Abby Sweet's motorcycle, on which she had attached a sidecar for Reggie. But, instead, he rode sitting behind her, after filling the side car with several boxes of fruit delicacies for the new animals.

"I hope I can still speak Aardvark!" he shouted over the din of the engine. "I've never even met an Okapi. Did you know they're related to Giraffes?"

"Yes!" she shouted, "and they have stripes on their legs, just like Zebras."

"Also, I'm kind of worried about speaking Elephant. The accent of the African Elephant with its bigger ears may be very different from that of an Indian Elephant. I've only spoken the Indian Elephant dialect before. Judging from Jobi Conn's e-mail, this Elephant Blomm could be a challenge!"

"I have every confidence you will communicate beautifully!" Abby Sweet said loudly, gunning the motor.

When they came to the stop light near Plitt's gas station on Nostril Way, Reggie was brooding. "I have a funny feeling. Something is strange about that e-mail."

"What kind of something?" Abby Sweet asked.

"I remember it read *'train comes to Lincoln Park one week from Friday.'* I wonder why the word *'Park'* is there. It should have been *'zoo.'*"

"I'm sure it just means that the train must park to let off the animals."

"Trains don't park, do they?" Reggie asked her. "Cars, buses and trucks park. Ships dock. Planes land. What do trains do?"

The traffic was very heavy on Ankle Avenue, around Lincoln Station. Abby Sweet's motorcycle got stuck behind a tour bus from the nearby community of Veronica Lake. Big Max Flommock and his son, Little Max were in the car next to the motorcycle. They had just come from the orthodontist where the boy had been fitted for metal braces.

"Hi, Reggie!" Little Max called out. "Can I have a piece of that fruit?" The boy smiled, showing Reggie a mouthful of gleaming metal and orange rubber bands that matched the color of his hair.

"Sure," Reggie shouted over the traffic noise and tossed him a juicy pink Honeycrisp apple. Flommock grabbed the apple out of Little Max's hand and threw it back to Reggie.

"Maxie can't eat apples for another eight months because of the new braces on his teeth, old timer. But thanks all the same."

"The next time you come to the cottage," Reggie told the boy, "I'll grind an apple in my blender for you. I'll mix it with a little yogurt and peach juice, and you'll drink the best thing in the world."

"Sounds great!" Little Max called. "Me and Bobby will come see you."

Before Reggie could say "Bobby and I!" the traffic cleared, and Abby Sweet's motorcycle finally made it to Lincoln Station, which was crowded with people from all over the county. A huge banner had been stretched across the entrance that read, *WELCOME AFRICAN ANIMALS*.

As the tightly-packed throng strolled to the platform to await the 3:49 train, Reggie spotted Bernie Moon.

"Hello, Bernie Moon!" Reggie shouted cheerfully.

"Howdy, Reggie. How's the retirement coming along?"

"Very well indeed, Bernie. Thanks to you I'm busier than an army of acrobatic Ants. You remember Abby Sweet here, don't you?"

"Of course," Moon answered brightly. He took her hand and looked deeply into her thick glasses for more than a few moments.

"I'm so sorry about your demotion," she told him in a sweet tone.

"Yeah, I really don't understand it. I thought I was doing a pretty darned good job reporting on corruption and criminals. Being relegated to the page ten gardening desk is going to be rather tame, I fear."

"Oh, Bernie!" Reggie exclaimed. "You have jumped to another completely wrong conclusion! Plants lead very exciting lives. Someday I will tell you about the clever mistletoe and how it has an agreement with the wind to spread its seeds to the most fertile ground. I will scare you with tales of the pitcher plant that eats insects—even small frogs! Or the poisonous deadly nightshade or mankiller jungle vines. Nature has more than her share of entertaining violence."

Bernie Moon looked surprised. "Really? Violence and mayhem in nature? That's interesting!"

## The Lincoln Zoo Rebellion

"I'll show you how to make plants grow healthier and bigger by playing them classical music, and by talking to them. I'll introduce you to a preacher whose prayers over vegetables make them grow so enormous, he wins County Fair prizes every year. And, if you wish, I'll show you medicinal plants that can cure anything that ails you."

"You're the best, Reggie," Bernie Moon beamed, "But I think I'd still rather write about wicked, evil people. I don't mean to disrespect plants, mind you." He reached into his pocket and extracted a white envelope. "By the way, this letter came to the newspaper, addressed to you."

Reggie opened the envelope, which revealed a crisp new $100 bill inside. The letter had been postmarked from the state capital, but there was no hint who had sent the money. A short note simply read: "Congratulations on your retirement, from a secret friend." *Hm,* Reggie thought. *This is very intriguing.*

Mayor Throttlebottom stood on a wooden platform on the train platform and fumbled in his pocket to find his welcoming speech. He tapped on the microphone to make sure the public address system was operating properly. "Testing, one, two, three," boomed over the speakers.

The 3:49 was right on time. It let out a blast of its multi-pitched whistle as it approached the station, and the Lincoln High School Marching Band and Glee Club broke into their off-key rendition of "Hail, Hail, the Gang's All Here." The crowd applauded, cheered, and strained their eyes to see the flatcars carrying the animal cages.

The train pulled into the station and squealed to a halt. The crowd gasped in unison. The flatcars were empty!

"Where are my animals?!" Throttlebottom loudly spoke into the microphone, which blasted out the speakers. Everyone plugged their ears with their fingers at the unbearable volume.

The train's engineer leaned out of the cab of the engine train. "I dropped 'em off in Chicago, I did. The shipping order specifically read *Lincoln Park Zoo* and Lincoln Park is in Chicago!"

"You idiot!" Throttlebottom exploded into the mike. "Those animals were meant for *our* zoo. *The Lincoln Zoo in Lincoln*!"

The engineer took offense at being called an idiot. So, he pulled a lever and blew out a loud, angry puff of hot, wet steam that drowned out the mayor.

The crowd groaned at the disappointing anti-climax of what was supposed to be a wonderful celebration. The Marching Band and Glee Club students shuffled quietly back to their buses. Every face looked like a sad mask.

Reggie looked at Abby Sweet. "Now, I'm really worried. Those animals have endured a long sea voyage. Then, at New York harbor, they had to suffer blood tests and other examinations of the health officials. Next, they had the terrifying experience of a train ride. I am very concerned about their wellbeing. We'd better try to sort this out. Come with me."

He took her hand, and they walked briskly in the direction of Throttlebottom, who was wiping the steam from the train off his face with a handkerchief and sipping "mouthwash" from his flask.

"Mr. Mayor!" Reggie called. "We have to do something about this terrible situation right now. I propose that Ms. Sweet and I board the 4:19 to Chicago and try to find our animals."

"Nonsense," Throttlebottom hissed. "It's obvious the director of the Lincoln Park Zoo has stolen them."

## The Lincoln Zoo Rebellion

"But sir," Abby Sweet implored, "Perhaps it was a simple error on the part of that Jobi fellow."

"That's ridiculous," Throttlebottom jeered. "He received our check for the animals. Our correct address is clearly printed in plain sight on the upper left-hand corner of the check! Here's what I think happened: the Lincoln Park Zoo has spies at the Chicago railway station. When a shipment of animals arrives, their animal-nappers just steal them. But if you want to go on some wild Goose chase, go. See if I care."

"Could you give us some money for train tickets?" Abby Sweet implored.

"Oh, all right, if you insist." Throttlebottom reached into his pocket and plucked out a crumbled twenty-dollar bill.

Abby Sweet grabbed it and ran to the ticket office to buy two second class tickets for Chicago. She and Reggie boarded the train with only a few minutes to spare. The train jerked forward, and with a blast of steam, they were on their way.

When they arrived at the station in Chicago an hour later, as soon as the train came to a stop, Reggie and Abby Sweet jumped onto the platform. Reggie, hoping the animals were still at the station, immediately howled the traditional greeting of Leopards in the wild. "Aaarohtmgglrt!!" He was thrilled to hear a plaintive response in the distance. "They're here!" he exclaimed. "Let's find them."

Carrying his box of treats, Reggie scooted down the platform in the direction of the sound of the Leopard with Abby Sweet following a few steps behind. Reggie stopped and yelled something in Elephant. A thundering trumpet sound came from the east and he tore off in that direction.

"I don't like the sound of that Elephant," he said to Abby Sweet, between huffs and puffs from running. "He must be extremely stressed out!"

Finally, they spotted the flatbed cars with the animals' cages on a side track. When they reached the cages, Abby Sweet saw obvious signs that the poor dears were suffering from extreme thirst. She found pails of water by a nearby water pump and brought them to the thirsty creatures as fast as she could. Reggie helped, of course. Then she examined each animal individually—and was horrified at their poor state of health.

"It's a crime the way animals are treated when they are shipped from place to place," she called to Reggie, who was rushing from cage to cage, saying a few words to each of the surprised animals who, of course, had never before been addressed in their own languages by a human animal. He gave each of them a delicacy from his box of goodies, which created a much happier mood.

He came to the Gorilla cage. Inside, a 250-pound female with a thick black coat, sat with the most confused look on her face. He greeted her in the Eastern Lowland Gorilla dialect. Happy to hear a familiar sound, she thumped her chest and responded with a deep growl, then pointed at a large pineapple in the corner of the cage.

"How strange!" Reggie called to Abby Sweet, pointing to the fruit. "This Gorilla says that the pineapple over there is not really a pineapple. What else could it be?"

Reggie saw something shocking to the senses. The pineapple "stood up" and began waddling across the cage toward them.

Abby Sweet ran over to see what was going on. "What in the blazes is that?" she exclaimed.

"I think it must be an animal trapped inside a rather large pineapple," Reggie said.

"Excuse me, sir. I'm very hot and tired," the pineapple said in a very un-pineapple voice. "Can you let me out of the cage now, please?"

Reggie's eyes popped. "Holy Hedgehogs! You spoke to me in English! I didn't know that pineapples could talk, much less speak English!"

"Of course. I speak perfect English and excellent Swahili and Bantu, as well," the pineapple explained in a young boy's voice, and began to shed some of the pineapple costume by removing the face mask with the leafy branches of the pineapple's crown. The pineapple's head introduced itself. "My name is Peter Nelson N'gara. I'm thirteen years old. I stowed away on the ship all the way from Africa."

Then he fainted. The poor boy was dehydrated, like the rest of the animals.

Abby Sweet immediately poured great washes of fresh, cool water on Peter's face and smaller squirts into his dry mouth. His eyes fluttered open, said "thank you," and closed again.

It took four hours to haul the animals back to the Lincoln Zoo from Chicago and place them in cages. Reggie and Abby Sweet agreed that there was a lot of work to be done to restore health and happiness to the suffering creatures.

## Chapter Eleven

For two whole days, Peter slept soundly on the convertible sofa in the living room of Reggie's cottage, suffering from acute exhaustion. He had been running a high fever. Abby Sweet called on him three times a day and treated him with cold compresses and shots of antibiotics. Louie, the Lemur, stayed with him every minute to make sure the compresses didn't slip off of his forehead.

Peter woke up only once, took one look at Louie, and passed out again.

The new animals were suffering, too. Many of them had severe dehydration, which caused faintness, rapid pulse, nausea, and vomiting. Some of them were weak from starvation. Reggie was relieved that Abby Sweet was so knowledgeable about medications for animals. Together, they fed the poor creatures vitamin supplements, minerals, and special nutrients to bring them back to their normal feeding patterns.

Reggie implored Mayor Throttlebottom to close the zoo for two weeks for the sake of the new animals, but the mayor would not agree. "The zoo will reopen next Saturday and that's my final decision!" he insisted, burping loudly.

In his conversations with the animals, Reggie learned that no vet or animal handler had traveled with them on their terrible sea journey. Storms and high seas caused much seasickness and several of them thought they were going to die.

"It wouldn't have been so awful if we each had another of our species to talk with and just be around," grunted Fingers, a Pygmy Chimpanzee. Reggie had no trouble understanding. The Chimp had been born with one oddly shaped hand, hence his name, "Fingers." Reggie liked him immediately and the feeling was mutual.

Likewise, Reggie struck up an immediate rapport with Dirk, the Yellow Baboon, and learned why he jumped into Jobi Conn's truck and decided to stay there. He had been disappointed when he was rejected by a female in his troop—which is what they call a group of Baboons—and welcomed the thought of travel to a far-off land where he might find a mate.

The Eastern Gorilla, whose name sounded something like "Emala," told Reggie as much as she knew about the boy, Peter. "My cage was next in line to be loaded on to the ship when suddenly the door opened and the creature came in wearing this strange pineapple costume," she explained. "The pineapple was very frightened of me and spent the entire journey huddled in the far corner of the cage. Its fear smelled bad. Why are human animals so afraid of us Gorillas? Don't they know we are harmless, loving creatures? We don't even eat other animals!"

Reggie was unable to speak any words of Okapi, which he found extremely disappointing. He tried squeaks, much like Sam the Giraffe occasionally makes since the two species are related, but it didn't work.

The language of the Spotted Hyena also gave him trouble. Although Hyenas appear more like Dogs, they are, in fact, more closely related to Cats. When he fed it for the first time, the animal "laughed" with a series of cackles, cries, and barks, but Reggie couldn't understand any of it. *I will find the key*, he promised himself, determined to figure out Hyena within a year.

Then, suddenly, a brain wave entered his head with the words, "I can teach you!" It was one of the strongest brain waves Reggie had ever received without placing his hand on an animal's head. He stared deep into the black eyes of the Hyena. "Is that you?" he mind-projected.

"Yes of course it is," the Hyena cackled, and Reggie understood! This was indeed a marvelous turn of events.

Then Reggie visited the Black Rhino, who was extremely upset because the zoo contained no mud pit. Rhinos in the wild wallow in mud to help cool themselves and provide protection from biting insects. During dry seasons, they take dust baths.

The Rhino confided to Reggie that he felt much safer at Lincoln Zoo than in his homeland. In Central Africa, he had witnessed humans killing his cousins from the air, from a large, loud flying bird—a machine! After shooting them dead, sometimes with machine guns, the machine landed, and humans came out of them. They'd chop off the horns of the Rhinos and then get back into the bird and fly away, leaving the carcasses behind for Hyenas and Vultures. "Why does the human animal want our horns so badly?" the Rhino asked Reggie. "They are not so different from your own fingernails!"

Reggie was deeply embarrassed. How could he tell the Rhino about the folly of people in Eastern countries who believe a bit of powdered horn can stop fever and fill one with lusty energy? How could he explain that Arab artisans carve the horns into ornamental handles for daggers and sell them for a small fortune?

He decided to tell a white lie. "The human believes you are the strongest animal in the wild, so they think if they take your horns, they'll become strong too."

The Rhino grunted. "It will take more than a bit of horn to make the human animal more powerful than me."

Reggie tried to get to know Blomm, the African Elephant. He remembered that Jobi Conn O'Brien warned in his e-mail to be careful with Blomm. But he had no trouble communicating with the bulky Pachyderm. In fact, he found Blomm's African Elephant accent unusually similar to the Indian Elephant accent, which was quite surprising, considering they lived 3,500 miles apart from one another. Physically, they're pretty much alike. While African Elephants have two sensitive finger-like tips at the end of their trunks, the Indian Elephants have only one. Africans have very large ears, while the Indian's are much smaller, and have a higher forehead than the African. African Elephants seem to have longer legs. Still, one can tell at a glance that these cousins look very much alike.

When Reggie touched the Elephant's head, strange, violent images sprang into his mind. He received powerful brain waves of Elephants trampling innocent creatures and stomping on wooden tree branches. He began to think that perhaps he'd found an animal that he might never understand.

On the morning of the third day, Abby Sweet recoiled with surprise when she saw Reggie's kitchen table, laden with ten huge buttermilk pancakes, stacked high, next to a small mountain of scrambled eggs.

"What army have you invited to breakfast?" she asked.

"It's my theory that aromas of a sizzling breakfast can sometimes awaken feverish young boys," Abby Sweet explained.

They went into the living room, where Peter was still sleeping. The wonderful aromas of breakfast spoke strongly to their senses. Suddenly, the boy's eyelids fluttered, and he awoke with a start.

"Hello. My name is..."

"Peter Nelson N'gara," Reggie finished Peter's sentence. "Welcome to the land of the living."

"Uhm...where am I?" Peter stuttered.

"The bathroom is over there," Reggie pointed. "The bath is drawn, the towels are warm and Abby Sweet here has brought you some of her cast-off jeans, sneakers, and T-shirts emblazoned with the names Miley Cyrus, Jonas Brothers, Ariana Grande and other musical artistes that I hear are rather famous."

"Thanks!" Peter said enthusiastically and ran to the bathroom.

Abby Sweet had never seen any single human being eat as much breakfast as Peter consumed that morning. She and

Reggie were both burning with curiosity to learn how the boy had managed to stow away on the ship disguised as a pineapple, but they had to put those questions aside until he waded through the mound of food.

Finally, after his tenth pancake, he put down his fork, wiped his chin with a napkin and smiled. "I feel alive again! Thanks!"

"'Thanks' are quite unnecessary, my boy," Reggie assured him, "but an explanation of who you are, where you're from, and how you got here would be of great interest to Abby Sweet and myself."

Peter told them about his father falling out of favor with his country's dictator and his parents' arrest and imprisonment. He described how Jobi Conn gave him sanctuary at the wildlife rescue game reserve, and how the workers' illness created the need for him to join the animal's caravan to Mombasa to help out. He told them about the arrest of Joe Otoronga, which he heard about from the corridor in the customs building.

He explained: "When I heard the men pass by, I snuck out and ran down the corridor in the other direction. There was an exit to the street.

"I ran as fast as I could to Joe Otoronga's truck. I was going to try to drive it away, but the keys were missing. Behind the seat I found a bag of fruit costumes for the harvest festival. I grabbed it and ran to where the conveyor belt was moving the animals' cages onto the ship. I put on the pineapple outfit and slipped into the cage of the Gorilla.

Reggie and Abby Sweet listened with wide-eyed anticipation and wonder.

"As we waited for the ship to depart, I saw policemen combing the dock area and I shivered, thinking they must be looking for me. I think I even saw the same men who had come to arrest me at my parent's house. But finally, the ship let out a blast of its whistle and pulled away from the dock.

"And that's about it. The voyage was one long nightmare. The hold of the ship was next to the galley and frightful smells of all varieties of spices and animal droppings mixed together made me ill. The seamen often forgot to give the animals water. The storms at sea had me clinging to the bars for hours on end. I feared the Gorilla in my cage would attack me at any moment. I thought the journey would never end. And you know the rest."

Reggie was amazed. "That is one miraculous story. You are a very brave pineapple." Reggie smiled warmly. "I'm glad our lives have crossed. But now we must look to the future. I think I should send an e-mail to Jobi Conn O'Brien and advise him that you are here. He must be terribly worried!"

"Please don't!" Peter implored. "That could bring him terrible trouble from the local police! They are surely hacking into Jobi's e-mails."

Reggie thought for a moment. "Perhaps there is a way." He went over to his desk and opened his MacBook computer and began typing furiously. "How's this?" he asked Peter.

*From: reggie@thelincolnzoo.org*

*To: Jobi Conn O'Brien. Central African Mbinguni Game Reserve. All animals arrived safely, including an unexpected surprise. Please give my best regards to Kafi, Evaristo, Mitch and the giant, Curly, with hopes they make a quick recovery from their tummy ailments, and I pray for the safety of Joe Otoronga. We are concerned about the Elephant Blomm, but especially pleased to have an Okapi and Lowland Gorilla. Yours sincerely, Reggie, retired zookeeper, Lincoln Zoo.*

"That's brilliant!" Peter exclaimed. "No one else could have told you about the men being sick except me!"

"I am glad you approve," Reggie beamed with satisfaction.

"But I am curious why you have capitalized the breeds of the animals in your e-mail," Peter asked. "I have never seen this done before."

"I have always done it. It gives them the respect they deserve," Reggie said. "Why should Swedish people, Chinese, Lithuanians, Zimbabweans, and Americans be capitalized and not Groundhogs, Warthogs and Hedgehogs?"

"Then I will do so, too," declared Peter.

"But more importantly, we must start thinking about your future. I suggest you remain here at the zoo with me, and we'll enroll you at the Lincoln Hills Middle School in the fall."

"I'm sure my parents would approve, sir," Peter replied, "But I have no funds to pay for my board and lodging or even the splendid breakfast you have just given me."

"Well, first of all, don't call me 'sir.' Just 'Reggie' will do. And money is the least of your problems. The Board of Directors promised me an assistant and they haven't hired one yet. Would you like to work with animals?"

"Uhm, I don't think they particularly like me, uh...Reggie."

"You're certainly wrong there," chuckled the zookeeper with an impish twinkle in his eye. "I happen to know that you made a good impression on them. In fact, I know one animal that wishes you were friendlier to her on the boat!"

Reggie and Abby Sweet took Peter on their rounds and showed him the attractions of Lincoln Zoo. To his credit, the boy was more interested in the animals than the video game arcade, bowling alley, merry-go-round, and other games and rides. "I've never heard of a zoo where the toy store was the biggest thing of all," Peter said.

The next day, the zoo directors came around to inspect the new animals. When Reggie spotted them approaching, he asked Abby Sweet to remove Peter to the veterinary surgery building and keep him out of sight. She pointed out that there was a hidden room in the surgery building behind the animal cages. "I can set up a bed for him there."

Reggie was concerned because the boy was an undocumented immigrant without a passport or identity papers. The US government had recently clamped down on such people, often referred to as 'illegal aliens,' and had been deporting many of them back to their home countries, especially Mexico and Central America. Reggie would have to figure out a way to get Peter proper documents to allow him to stay in America.

"You're not an alien," Reggie told Peter. "You're not from outer space, are you?"

"Certainly not," replied Peter.

"But please listen carefully. If ever I feel you are in any danger, I will make the traditional call of Lowland Gorillas in the wild, which means I want you to run and hide. Okay?"

"Sure. What does that sound like?" asked Peter.

"Like this!" Reggie opened his mouth wide and emitted a loud sound that sounded like "Ahhkecccht okk. Ahhkecccht okkee."

"Wow," Peter said, clamping his hands to his ears. "That's the most ear-splitting noise I've ever heard! How did you learn to do that?"

Reggie smiled. "Perhaps I'll tell you about it one day, young fella, but we need to get better acquainted."

## Chapter Twelve

The next night—a moonless night—Blomm dragged his massive forelegs back and forth, gradually digging a sizable hole in the soil of his caged enclosure. Striking rock, he trampled the earth furiously and angrily heaved his enormous six-ton bulk at the bars of the cage. They wouldn't give.

His head was buzzing. The tissue around his six-foot long tusks became inflamed. Small glands between his eyes and mouth began secreting a dark green, oily substance. He was in a state of "musth," which occurred in male Elephants. He felt claustrophobic—the terrifying fear of being in an enclosed place. He had to run. But he was surrounded by the bars of his cage. No problem. He had the ability to use his trunk to help him escape.

An Elephant's trunk is a most remarkable appendage. It is a combination nose, hand, tool, food and water collector, and weapon. It can pluck a single leaf or berry from a tree or carry a giant log. It can suck up two gallons of water at a time and can detect smells over two miles away. It has over 40,000 muscles in it.

Blomm felt each bar of his cage with the sensitive double finger-like tips at the end of his trunk. Several bars in the corner seemed different than others. They seemed flimsy…or, at least, flimsy to an Elephant. He grasped one of them and twisted with his muscular trunk. The top half snapped off like a peppermint candy cane.

He dropped it to the ground outside the cage, then snapped off another. Then a third and fourth, and so on, until only a few feet of bar were left sticking up at the bottom.

Gingerly, Blomm stepped over the stumps of the bars and squeezed his way past them to the outside. It was pitch black, and since he was an Elephant, he was extremely near-sighted, even in the light, so he moved his bulky body slowly and tentatively down the path. He raised his trunk high in the air, smelling for danger.

## The Lincoln Zoo Rebellion

The Aardvark (a nocturnal animal that sleeps all day and is active all night) looked up, startled, and then resumed burrowing for the ants and termites that Reggie had hidden in rotten logs of his cage. Blomm ambled past the Ostrich, as she continued sleeping soundly in a standing position, and then made his way past the cages of the new Monkey arrivals, Fingers, Dirk, and the Lowland Gorilla, Emala, without arousing them, and wandered into the main square.

He saw the water gushing from the Ralph Bear fountain and walked over to have a drink. He downed a gallon and a half with one long slurp of his trunk. Across the square, he smelled Lion; to the north, he smelled Rhino and Leopard. He couldn't sense an animal smell to the south, so he proceeded in that direction. After passing the veterinary surgery building, he became confused.

It felt like he was no longer out-of-doors, but rather inside some large, enclosed place. He slowly rotated in circles; his trunk extended. He felt a cold metallic object against his leg and examined it with his trunk. It felt like smooth glass and metal and had a slight buzzing sound and sensation. He lowered his trunk, reached under the object, and with a kick, he toppled it over. The Pac-Man Championship video game machine crashed to the cement floor with the noise of breaking glass and twisted metal.

Startled, he jumped backwards, and his tail swishing in the air, hit a main electricity switch. Colored lights flashed on, bells sounded, and a siren went off in the Angry Birds video game machine he had knocked to the floor, clicking off 39,000 points.

Blomm panicked and tore around the arcade, overturning machine after machine, collapsing each to the floor in an explosion of shattering glass, disgorging their electrical innards.

He stuck one of his tusks into the Captain Fantastic Machine and lashed out at Sonic the Hedgehog, which toppled on top of the Pirates of Monster Island. In the clatter of destruction, he felt panic.

He lurched wildly in all directions looking for a way out. Now, the shooting gallery was in his way, and he saw the row of air rifles that children used to shoot at cartoon animal targets. He had seen these exploding branches before in Africa. In fact, he had once been shot in the leg and he would never forget that trauma. The sight of those long wooden sticks drove him crazy.

Blomm went berserk, jamming his tusks into the table and toppling the rifles to the ground. He stomped on them and crunched them to a woody pulp. Then, head lowered, he charged against the central pillar of the video game arcade and the whole building swayed. He hit it again. It swayed even more.

For a brief moment, he paused and smelled a smell so awful he knew instinctively that he had to leave the area immediately. The piercing odor of an electrical fire burned his senses. He heaved his bulk against the central pillar and ran in the only direction he hadn't yet tried, and suddenly slipped through the archway to the outside world. With a thundering convulsion, the entire roof caved in on top of the wreckage of the arcade machines and erupted in flames.

Blomm narrowly missed the ticket booth by inches as he stormed ahead, then crashed through the gates and charged down Lincoln Zoo Road. Fortunately, there was no traffic in the pitch-black night, so after several hundred feet, he slowed his pace. Although there were no familiar smells of the African bush, he felt free.

## The Lincoln Zoo Rebellion

Reggie's eyes popped open. *What was that?* He sensed something was dreadfully amiss. He sat upright in bed and pushed the rod that opened the window in his roof, right above his bed. He sniffed the air. *Uh oh!*

He threw off the covers, stood on top of the bed, and looked out the window. His eyes widened when he saw the sinister orange glow beyond the swimming pool.

In one fluid motion, he jumped to the floor, descended the rickety steps of the sleeping platform, seized the telephone and dialed 911. "We have a fire at Lincoln Zoo!" he cried into the receiver. "How fast can help get here?"

"As fast as we can, Reggie," replied the operator, a former childhood friend who recognized his voice.

"That's not fast enough!" Reggie exclaimed. "I'm going to have to do something myself!" He hung up the phone, grabbed his toolbox, and ran out the door. He ran surprisingly fast to the veterinary surgery building where Peter was sleeping and banged on the door while yelling for Peter to wake up and meet him at the swimming pool.

At the swimming pool, Reggie's heart sank at the sight of the burning arcade. He frantically turned on the hose used to clean the deck and stretched it as far as it would go, but the water pressure wasn't strong enough to shoot as far as the arcade. Peter arrived and felt helpless as he watched Reggie activate all the filters and pumps. Taking spanners from his toolbox, the old zookeeper patched the pumps and filters together in a clever way so that it sucked water from the swimming pool backwards into a pump that fed the hose.

He yelled to Peter to carry the hose towards the arcade. "Either we'll have enough pressure to put out this blaze or I'll blow all the pipes from here to kingdom come," he cried.

When Peter got as close as he could get to the arcade, Reggie turned the valve sharply to a wide-open position. Water surged from the swimming pool, through the re-routed valves and pump and out of the hose with such force that Peter was thrown to the ground. The hose twisted and swung about like a dancing Snake, water spurting everywhere. Reggie ran to help, and together they managed to secure the runaway hose and concentrate the water on the flames.

"The pipes are holding!" Reggie smiled at Peter. "I hope the fire engines get here soon. Otherwise, the Scouts may not have any water for their water polo game tomorrow!"

Just then, Reggie spotted Fingers, the Pygmy Chimpanzee, swaying down the path. His lips were puckered as he bobbed his head up and down. Reggie called to him in Chimpanzee. "How did you get out of your cage?"

"Nothing to it," Fingers said. "I snapped two of the bars off like the dead twigs of an African Tulip Tree." The Chimp joined in to help Reggie and Peter aim the water on the burning arcade. Peter wondered what in the world Reggie was saying to the Chimp as the old zookeeper communicated in hoots and clicks and made broad facial expressions. Peter had never heard sounds like this before from a person's mouth or seen such animated facial language from a human.

Meanwhile, Blomm continued briskly down Lincoln Zoo Road, following the streetlights in the distance until he heard the sounds of approaching sirens. He turned off the road to the south and rambled through an old cemetery, inadvertently knocking a dozen gravestones to the ground.

The lumbering Elephant then stopped at a fruit orchard long enough to devour the greater part of a delicious peach tree as the fire engines sped past him, followed by several police cars with their sirens blazing—including Chief of Police, Grant Buxton. A small red sports car followed the police cars. Behind the wheel sat Bernie Moon, on a mission. Bernie, despite his demotion to gardening writer, continued to chase fires and scandalous stories that he hoped would get him on local TV.

After the emergency vehicles—and Bernie Moon—passed, Blomm came out of the trees, crossed the road down Funny Bone Street and ambled south. He saw colorful lights in the distance and headed towards them.

The lights became more brilliant as they reflected a thousand-fold on glistening metal vehicles below them. Colorful flags waving in the breeze came into his line of vision on which were printed the words BEAUTIFUL BEETLE, JAZZY JAGUAR, FAB RABBIT, PHANCY PANTHER, CRAZY COUGAR, IMPRESSIVE IMPALA, POWERFUL PINTO, and MARVELOUS MUSTANG.

Blomm had arrived at Big Max's used car lot, owned by zoo president, Max Flommock, but to the Elephant all *he* saw was just another group of machines that made him angry.

He lunged at the IMPRESSIVE IMPALA and impaled it with his huge tusks. He toppled it over onto the convertible roof of the CRAZY COUGAR, which blew out its tires and shot its radiator and headlights over to the middle of Elbow Place. He stomped on the two cars again and again, pulverizing them into the ground, sending various pieces sailing into the air. He mangled the hood of the PHANCY PANTHER and pounced on the POWERFUL PINTO. With super Elephantine strength, he picked up the rear end of the MARVELOUS MUSTANG by its back bumper and hurled it against the JAZZY JAGUAR, which collapsed in a heap, its horn blaring.

Blomm grew tired of this game. He gave a few cursory kicks at a Colt, which sent its hubcaps rolling down the street and its fenders flying through the plate glass window of the showroom. Surprisingly, the tension began to leave his mind and body. He wandered down the street towards Town Hall, flapping his ears to cool himself, and trumpeted a call of joy.

Abby Sweet jumped out of bed. *What was that?* She found her thick glasses, put them on, and ran to the window. She peered down Kneecap Lane in the next block, and saw Blomm the Elephant, nibbling some newly mown grass in front of The Bedside Manor Retirement Home.

Abby Sweet lived in a rented room above the Small Planet Coffee Shop, run by a widow named Emma Jean Likorisch, who lived in the apartment below her. After throwing on her clothes she ran down the stairs and banged on Mrs. Likorisch's door. "There's an Elephant loose," she explained, "and I need some fruit to keep him calm. May I please have the keys to the coffee shop?"

"Oh, goody," the excited Mrs. Likorisch cried, "I love Elephants."

"You wouldn't love this one," Abby Sweet warned. "Stay in your apartment and lock the door. And please call Reggie at the zoo and ask him to come here as soon as possible!"

The young vet gathered a box full of fruit from the Small Planet Coffee Shop, including plums, pears, and nectarines, and dragged the carton to the pavement outside. Mrs. Likorisch leaned out of her window. "Abby dear, there is no answer at Reggie's cottage."

How many times did you let it ring?" Abby Sweet asked.

"At least ten."

Abby Sweet gulped. *I guess I'm on my own*, she thought to herself. She looked across the street. The Elephant had wandered down to Town Hall, where he went about digging up the flower beds. Abby could almost hear his ears flapping back and forth. She tried to remember if that indicates that an Elephant is agitated or if he is trying to cool itself down. She decided that cooling down was the answer and went back inside the coffee shop to find some ice cream.

She took a large tub from the freezer—making a mental note to reimburse Mrs. Likorisch—and carried it to the door. When she swung it open to leave, she found herself face to trunk with Blomm.

"Oops."

Abby Sweet took a little jump backwards and then got up her courage. She straightened up and looked Blomm right in the face. "Well, you are a clever fellow to be able to escape from our zoo, aren't you?" she murmured in a slow, level voice.

She dipped her hand into some soft vanilla ice cream and held it to the end of his trunk. He sniffed her hand tentatively, then placed the sweet goodness in his mouth. The vanilla ice cream was cold and refreshing. He held his trunk out for more.

Abby Sweet then turned and started walking up the road towards the zoo. Blomm followed her. At every corner she gave him another scoop of ice cream and a piece of fruit, until he had eaten it all. Then, to her surprise, Blomm kneeled down on one leg, wrapped his trunk around her waist, and gently lifted her onto his back. When they arrived at the zoo she was shocked to see the fire engines, police cars, and the smoldering remains of what used to be the video arcade.

Abby Sweet tickled the Elephant's ear. "You have really done some mischief this time, Mr. Blomm."

The Elephant bellowed in agreement.

## Chapter Thirteen

A few minutes after Blomm's attack, Max Flommock was awakened by his telephone ringing insistently. It was a man who lived next door. "Your car lot has been smashed to smithereens, Flommock! You'd better have good insurance because one of your bumpers came flying through my window and almost brained me!"

Shaken by the phone call, Flommock hurried to his car lot and surveyed the wreckage of his property. His heart sank. Not one car was salvageable. There was nothing he could do to fix things that late at night, so he returned home and went straight to his den, where he kept his business records. He took out his insurance file and quickly read it. *Oh, no!* He discovered that his premium payment was eighteen days overdue. He pored over his account books and then, at the crack of dawn, added up the figures. He was flat broke. He sat staring into space until the sound of the *Examiner* newspaper landing on his front steps snapped him out of his reverie.

He went outside and took a deep gulp of fresh morning air. He picked up the newspaper and carried it into the breakfast room. The headline read: WILDCAT STRIKE HITS TOY FACTORY. The text said that the employees who stuffed the wildcat dolls were only getting a half hour for lunch, while the Ralph Bear stuffers were getting a whole hour. To make matters worse, a man named Edward Eugene Pincus of U.S. ICE (U.S. Immigration and Customs Enforcement) was investigating the toy factory to make certain no illegal Mexican workers were employed there. Flommock frowned. He knew there were quite a few of them on the job.

"Oh dear," Flommock mumbled to himself. "This is going to put Ralph in a terrible mood." Then he saw an article that made him shudder.

## The Lincoln Zoo Rebellion

### ZOO VIDEO ARCADE DESTROYED

By our gardening correspondent, Bernie Moon

Late last night, the video game arcade at the zoo was razed to the ground and caught fire. The cause of the destruction has not been determined, according to Police Chief Grant Buxton.

Flowers and shrubs were smashed, including several rare lilies and orchids. The fire did not destroy any trees, however, but it did singe a few bushes near the veterinary surgery building. Long-lashed veterinarian, Abby Sweet was not there at the time, much to the disappointment of this correspondent.

Firemen on the scene credit retired zookeeper, Reggie Goodenough, and an unknown youth wearing a rock 'n roll T-shirt, with putting out the blaze before it spread to adjoining buildings.

Despite the destruction of the arcade, the reopening of the zoo and debut of the new African animals will go ahead next Saturday as planned, promised Board Chairman Ralph Throttlebottom.

Flommock looked at his insurance file again, his eyes wide with shock. He realized the worst: *Insurance had not been obtained for any of the new buildings at the zoo!* He had even forgotten to give secretary-treasurer, Howard Plitt, the paperwork to insure the new animals. "What a revolting development this is!" he exclaimed loudly, knowing full well it was his own fault.

Flommock was certain that when Throttlebottom discovered his error, the mayor would boot him off the board and stop his Zoo Director's salary, which was all he had left. There was only one thing to do. He would have to beg Throttlebottom to forgive him.

"G'morning, dad! How ya doin'?" Little Max called from the stairs. "I just heard on my radio that the video game arcade got wrecked last night."

"I know, Maxie."

"Can I go over there right now?" the boy asked eagerly. "I bet I can find lots of quarters that spilled out of the broken machines. I'll be rich!"

"All right. I need to go there myself..." Big Max answered. *And face the music*, he thought to himself. "Go brush your braces first, Maxie."

Little Max Flommock stomped around in the burned-out arcade and his clothes became filthy. He was disappointed to only find ten quarters in the debris because most of the coins had been removed from the machines before Blomm did his damage. He walked down the path to the playground where he spied a strange boy sitting on one end of a seesaw, lost in thought.

Little Max walked over to him and extended his hand. "Hi, I'm the son of the zoo president."

Peter shook his hand. "How do you do? I'm the son of the Minister of Tourism."

"That's stupid," Little Max scoffed. "We have a minister at our church, but a tourism minister sounds silly."

"Well, I assure you there is such a job title, but they don't have to be religious."

"What are you doing here anyway?" Little Max asked. "The zoo doesn't open until Saturday."

"I work for Mr. Reggie," Peter answered.

"Hey, that's great. I like Reggie, but my dad calls him a geezer. I don't know what that means. Do you?"

"Of course," answered Peter. "A geezer is what snobby British people sometimes call men of a very mature age. My friend Jobi Conn uses it sometimes, but just in fun like when he says, 'For a little boy, you're just a bloody old geezer!' Reggie may look older, but he's got tremendous energy. I helped him put out the fire last night. Do you come from around here?"

"Naw, I was born in Peanut, California," Little Max said. "How 'bout you?"

"I was born in Africa."

"Really? Wow!" Little Max exclaimed. "That's even further away than California! How did you get here?"

"I came with the new animals, on a ship from a place called Mombasa. My name is Peter. What's yours?"

"My mom and dad call me Little Max because my dad is Big Max. But some people call me Carrot-top."

"I can see why!" Peter smiled. "Your hair is certainly bright red! I'm thirteen. How old are you, Carrot-top?"

"I'm twelve, Pete. My dad is the president of the zoo and he owns a used car lot, but it got messed up last night by your Elephant."

"I'm really sorry about that," Peter apologized.

"I guess it ain't your fault," Little Max shrugged. "Did your parents bring you on the boat?"

"No. They're both in jail back in Africa," Peter replied.

"No kidding! Wow! I never knew anybody in jail before. Did they kill somebody?"

"No, it's a long story. I'll tell it to you if you promise to keep it secret. I don't think people are supposed to know I am here."

"I swear on a stack of bibles," Little Max promised. "I won't even tell my best friend, Bobby, and I'll share the quarters I found in the arcade with you."

Peter proceeded to tell the whole story to Little Max, who was fascinated to learn about Jobi Conn, Joe Otoronga, and especially the part about sharing a cage on the sea voyage with a Lowland Gorilla.

"That's the most incredible story I've ever heard, Pete!" Little Max exclaimed, handing over four quarters. "Would you show me your pineapple costume someday?"

"Sure."

Little Max had an idea. "What are you doing Saturday afternoon? After the zoo reopens, me and some of the kids are going bowling."

"I've never been inside a bowling alley," Peter admitted. "But I love playing tennis."

"You don't know how to bowl? Wow, it's the greatest game. I'll teach you how to bowl if you teach me tennis?"

"Sure," answered Peter. "It'll be interesting to meet some other kids too."

"Let's meet at the snack shop for lunch, 'cause we have to wait until the Woman's Team finishes their bowling match."

Meanwhile in the zoo's office building Reggie sat on a bench in the hallway waiting for his meeting with the mayor. He thought

## The Lincoln Zoo Rebellion

hard about the best way to tell him about the faulty cages and how the Elephant was able to get free and his fears that the other animals would soon discover the weaknesses of the cages too. But he had to wait until the mayor was finished speaking with zoo president, Big Max Flommock.

Flommock, down on his knees before the glowering mayor, whined. "It was the Elephant, Ralph. It got loose and trampled the arcade and my used car lot. And neither of them were insured! Can you ever forgive me?"

"Ah, Max, Max, Max," Throttlebottom sighed. "Normally a gross blunder like not obtaining insurance would be grounds for immediate dismissal."

"I'm throwing myself on your mercy, Ralph." Flommock looked up at the mayor with the saddest, most hopeful expression.

The big man smiled down at Flommock. "Perhaps I can help. I have three Cadillacs and I only need one of them. You may put the other two on your demolished used car lot and rent them out. We'll split the profits."

Flommock brushed a tear of relief from his eye. "That would be amazing, Ralph! Maybe I could also start a limousine service and drive rich people around myself. I could buy a uniform and a cap. I could even drive you!"

"An excellent idea, Max! There are several limos sitting in the garage at my toy factory."

Big Max Flommock stood up and shook Throttlebottom's hand over and over. "How can I thank you, Ralph? You've saved my life! I'll always be loyal to you."

"You'd better be!" The mayor slapped Flommock on the back and pushed him out the door to the corridor. In the hallway, Reggie stood up, ready for his own meeting with the Mayor.

"I'll be with you right after I make a few calls, gramps!" Throttlebottom yelled to the zookeeper through the open door.

"Harold G. Koonin please," bellowed the mayor into the phone. The name rang a bell to Reggie. Then he remembered the article identifying Koonin as the Canadian banker who heads the *Examiner* syndicate. Why would Throttlebottom be talking to him?

"Yo, Hal. Our new editor printed a front-page story today that I don't like. Tell him not to print any more nasty pieces about labor problems at my factory. And for God's sake, don't let on that I'm the secret owner, okay? (MAYOR PAUSES) Thanks Hal. Give my best to your wife, Judy."

*So that was it!* Reggie thought to himself, his face red with anger. *Throttlebottom bought the newspaper himself after Bernie Moon's article appeared about the Board trying to fire me! This is disgraceful!*

Throttlebottom made another telephone call, ordering insurance on the video game arcade and other new zoo attractions. The mayor demanded that the start of the policy be backdated, which made Reggie's face turned even redder.

*I can't believe it,* he muttered to himself. *Would he dare to make an insurance claim for the destruction of the video game arcade even though it wasn't insured? That is outrageously dishonest! I'm getting extremely mad now.*

Finally, Throttlebottom spun around in his swivel chair and gestured to Reggie to come in. "How's your retirement going, old timer?" he said robustly.

"Not very well, two-timer," Reggie snapped angrily. "Just because I'm of an advanced age, doesn't mean I don't hear things. I am not deaf. I heard every word you just said on the phone and I think your behavior is abominable. You are trying to manipulate public information in this town by buying the newspaper and you are about to commit insurance fraud!"

"You don't know what you're talking about," the mayor shrugged.

Reggie continued, "I've been quiet too long. I've got some very angry animals on my hands, especially the new ones—including the Elephant who destroyed your precious video arcade. I demand better living conditions for them. Many of the new cages are faulty due to cheap building materials. We must tear them down and build new habitats. The whole zoo must be reorganized!"

"Calm down," the mayor consoled. "Take a seat. Let's talk this over, man-to-man."

"I will *not* calm down," Reggie growled. "Something must be done immediately. If not, I may have to call the police!"

"They won't listen to you, Pops," Throttlebottom snapped angrily. "You are a penniless, retired zookeeper. I am the rich Chairman of the Board, Mayor of the town, and largest employer in any city within a hundred-mile radius. The police chief, Grant Buxton, is a close personal friend of mine. I am powerfully connected! Now get your retired old butt outa here and behave yourself! We're going to re-open the zoo Saturday morning and that's that!"

Reggie glared at him. "You've already got one strike on your hands at the toy factory and now you're going to have another one right here at this zoo. I, myself, will go on strike and I will take the animals out on strike with me."

Throttlebottom exploded with laughter. He hit the sides of his pot belly, then banged the table in front of him so hard his pens and pencils hopped around like Mexican jumping beans. Pointing his finger at Reggie, he boomed, "He's retired but he's going on strike? That's rich!" The Mayor began to wheeze hysterically. "And he's taking the animals on strike with him! That kills me!" Throttlebottom pulled a handkerchief from his pocket and wiped away tears of laughter that had flooded his eyes.

"I suggest you call a meeting of the Board of Directors as soon as possible," Reggie demanded. "I suggest that Saturday, after the zoo reopens, would be an appropriate time and I will deliver our strike demands then and there." He turned around briskly and stormed out of the room.

Throttlebottom's laughter subsided to controlled giggling. He picked up the telephone.

"Chief of Police, Grant Buxton, please. Buxton? I'm glad I reached you. This is an emergency. I need a large team of police on alert Saturday morning when we re-open the zoo. We may have a problem with some faulty cages, so make sure your men are armed with loaded weapons, in case some of the animals escape.

"Oh, and Buxton," he sputtered, "I'm going to need a court order to remove a certain retired zookeeper from the premises on the grounds of obstruction of a public business. He's mad as a Snake. He actually threatened to take the animals out on strike, would you believe? He has to leave by Saturday, when the zoo reopens. So get going and get me that court order!"

That afternoon, Reggie bicycled over to the town library. He was surprised to find Peter there, reading a book by another Peter, an Australian philosopher named Peter Singer.

"What are you reading, my boy?" Reggie whispered, so as not to disturb any of the other readers.

"This is a great book called '*Animal Liberation*,'" Peter whispered back. "You would love it. It's all about how animals deserve to be given enough food and water and space to roam the earth without fear of being hunted. And he shows how if everyone ate a few less animals every year, no one in the whole world would go hungry!"

"That certainly sounds like my kind of book!" Reggie declared. But first I need to read about strikes. I have decided that we must go on strike for our animals."

"Why is that?" asked Peter.

"I think it may be the only way to change people's minds about what is really important in a zoo. The question is, what kind of strike should we do? A slow-down strike? A sick-out? A boycott or vigil or picket or march or general strike? Maybe a rally? Or something else."

Reggie went to the bookshelf and pulled out a book about the great East Indian leader, Mohandas Gandhi, who was better known as "Mahatma," which means "great soul." One of Gandhi's most effective protest methods was fasting. He wouldn't eat any food for days on end and only have an occasional few sips of water. He called it a "hunger strike" and it got him publicity around the world.

"If Gandhi could stop a riot in India by not eating, maybe I can stop the injustice at our zoo the same way," he told Peter.

"I know how hard it was not to eat and only sometimes drink anything for days when I was on the ship," Peter replied. "Are you certain you will be alright?"

"Trust me, my friend. It could get us the press coverage we need, just like it did for Gandhi. I will call Bernie Moon when I get home and see if he can put me and some of the animals on his TV show."

When he got back to his cottage, Reggie dialed Bernie Moon's home number. "Hello! Moon here," a voice answered.

"Hi Bernie Moon, this is Reggie, zookeeper. I've got a really hot story for you..."

But the voice on the other end did not stop talking. "Please don't hang up. I don't expect to be back for several weeks 'cause I'm working on a scoop, so leave your number and I'll call you back soon."

*Ugh!* Reggie realized that he was speaking to Bernie's answering machine. So he left a message. "Bernie! This is your friend Reggie. The zookeeper. I intend to go on a hunger strike on Saturday, when the zoo reopens, and I'm going to get all the animals to go on strike, too. I don't know how I'm going to do it yet, but I'm fighting mad and I can't take it anymore. I hope you'll write an article and maybe put me on TV..."

Reggie's message was interrupted by a very long beeeep. Apparently, Bernie Moon's answering machine had run out of space and couldn't take any more of his message. *I wonder where he is,* Reggie thought, as he yawned. *Maybe a nap would give me some ideas*, he mused to himself. So he curled up on the sofa and fell asleep in a jiffy.

## The Lincoln Zoo Rebellion

Reggie dreamed as he'd never dreamed before.

*His dream was tinged with a beautiful violet-blue hue and was accompanied by the music of Tibetan mountain pipes with a deep resonant 'toodeloo' sound. Reggie was riding his bicycle down to the gates of the zoo. Everyone was dressed in white, including Reggie himself.*

Thousands of children were waiting eagerly to see the new animals that had just arrived from Africa, but Reggie pedaled right past them, ignoring them all as he rode down Lincoln Zoo Road.

Little Max Flommock called after him. "Reggie! Come back! All is forgiven!"

"No deal!" Reggie called out. "I'm on strike! So are all the animals. We're on a sit-down strike. You'll see!" He continued his ride towards town.

"What is a sit-down strike?" Little Max asked Bobby Winkleman. "We'd better go see." The two of them then raced in slow motion to the cage of the new Rhinoceros. The huge animal was frozen like a statue. Flies buzzed around his face, but he made no attempt to whisk them away.

'I think this stupid Rhino is stone dead," Little Max said. "He's no fun at all."

Milt the Tiger stood in a state of suspended animation, his tail pointing straight out from his body like an Irish Setter that had just spotted a Pheasant. The new female Wildebeest had sunk its lyre-shaped horns in the dirt in front of him. The Chimpanzee, Baboon, and Marmoset sat together on the ground, their hands covering their eyes, ears, and mouth, respectively. Just like the three monkeys in the famous cartoon of "see no evil, hear no evil, speak no evil."

*Emala, the Lowland Gorilla, hung on the bars of her cage with her legs spread apart and arms outstretched. Goliath lay flat on his back with all four feet pointed straight up in the air. Leslie Wolf sat in a chair with his legs crossed, smoking a cigar, and Durante, the Proboscis Monkey, had his head stuck between his legs with his giant nose sticking out from under his bottom.*

*Every animal was completely motionless, as stiff as statues, with eyes staring out at the children.*

"What's going on?!" zoo president Max Flommock cried, rushing up to his son.

"The animals are on a sit-down strike, Dad, to try to get better living conditions. Reggie made them do it!"

"Son, they can't go on a sit-down strike," Flommock blubbered. "They're not even members of a union, son! I'd better go tell the mayor."

Flommock burst into the conference room at the office building. There sat Throttlebottom, Winkleman. and Plitt, dressed in white linen suits, counting piles of hundred-dollar bills.

"Men, we've got a strike on our hands! The animals have gone out, men." Flommock announced.

"What are you blathering about?" Throttlebottom yelled. "Animals can't picket. How would they hold up their signs?"

"They're not picketing, Ralph," Flommock whined, "They're on a sit-down strike."

"All of them?" Throttlebottom blustered.

"Every last mammal, bird, and reptile of them, Ralph, warned Flommock, "And to make things worse, Ralph, everyone at the zoo wants their money back!"

"Oh no!" the directors exclaimed in unison. "We can't give them back all their spondulicks!" They then started to gather up *the piles of paper money to hide in the closet, but a breeze came through the open window and tossed the notes into the air. The directors scrambled for the swirling money, crashing into each other, but the bills fluttered out of their hands and were sucked out the window into the square, where children calmly gathered them up and put them in their pockets.*

"Oh, yes!" Reggie sang out as he woke up with a smile on his face. *What a dream!* He sat up in bed and twirled his snow-white mustache. Then he laughed out loud. "A sit-down strike!" he said aloud. "That's a good one! That would leave out the Snails and giant Aldabra Turtles!"

Late that afternoon, Peter stopped by as usual to eat supper with Reggie, who had prepared his special sweet corn salad with green olives, scallions, and parsley in a lime cumin mayonnaise. Abby Sweet joined them, adding some deviled eggs and a cherry pie from Emma Jean Likorisch's shop to the meal.

"How was your day today, Peter?" Abby Sweet asked.

"Fine," he answered. "I met a carrot-top boy who invited me to meet all his friends at the bowling alley on Saturday."

"What a remarkable coincidence," exclaimed Reggie. "I just had a dream about the carrot top boy and his friend Bobby. I call them "the Devilish Duo" because they have very little respect for animals and are full of mischief. I have been very patient with them, but they don't seem to want to learn."

"Maybe I can speak to them, boy-to-boy. It wouldn't hurt, would it?" Peter suggested.

"Be very careful, Peter," Reggie said glumly. We don't want them talking about you until we solve the problem of how to get proper immigration papers." Peter decided not to tell Reggie that he had already disclosed the story of his escape from Mombassa to America to Little Max. He trusted his new red-haired friend, who was willing to swear on a stack of bibles.

After dinner, Peter and Abby Sweet joined Reggie on his evening rounds. They carried snacks to all the animals. By this time, Reggie had confided in Peter by demonstrating his ability to communicate with animals and telling how he learned to do that many years ago with the Canadian Red Fox named Hugh.

"I guessed that already," Peter admitted. "I have watched you often from the window and I see that sometimes you place your hands on an animal's head. My father always told me never to do that."

"Your father is right," Reggie agreed. "A Dog, for instance, might jump to the erroneous conclusion that you think you are his or her superior, and might bite or scratch you to prove you wrong. It is far better to gently stroke the Dog under the chin while smiling and saying, 'You're beautiful.' A smile sends the signal 'I do not wish you harm.' This works for people too—smiling that is, not the part about stroking them under the chin!"

They then visited Blomm. Reggie immediately apologized to him for the shackles he had placed on the Elephant's legs to make the Board believe he could not escape again.

He spoke with Dirk, Fingers, and Emala—the Baboon, Chimp, and Lowland Gorilla—and promised them that if he could find a way, he would find them mates. They pledged their help.

"We will come up with some ideas," Fingers told Reggie. "I am ready for love."

"I am ready for dinner," Emala mumbled, shoving a handful of bamboo shoots into her mouth.

The group spent some time with the Okapi and later the Leopard, a female, who told Reggie she wished to have an English name. He had no problem with that. He believed that giving animals names reminds people we are all part of the animal kingdom. He objected, however, when zookeepers gave ridiculous cutesy names like Babs Baboon, Andy Pandy or Gnancy Gnu.

"What would be a good English name for this beautiful Leopard?" Reggie asked Peter and Abby Sweet.

Abby Sweet thought for a minute. "We need a name that suggests glamour, beauty, and a person who believes in animal rights."

"I've got it!" Peter exclaimed. "Let's call her Lady Gaga!"

The Leopard was very pleased, indeed.

Reggie shared a joke with Sam the Giraffe, who quietly mooed like a Cow in response. He got into a playful argument with Goliath over who could growl the loudest.

Peter and Abby Sweet stayed with Reggie and the animals for almost two hours marveling at all the barking, bellowing, bleating, braying, cackling, clicking, croaking, gibbering, grunting, hissing, howling, humming, meowing, neighing, purring, quacking, roaring, screaming, snapping, snorting, trumpeting, whinnying, whistling, yelping, and yowling.

Abby Sweet carried her notebook with her and wrote down everything Reggie said about the animals' desires for improvements to the zoo. When she got home, she typed them into her computer and was surprised to see they were almost twenty pages long.

At the same time across town, Big Max Flommock tucked his son Little Max into bed and asked about his day.

"I can't tell you, Dad. I've sworn on a stack of bibles."

"You must not keep any secrets from your father, son, or he will probably have to withhold your allowance."

Little Max thought for a moment. "Well, if you promise not to tell anybody…"

"Don't worry son," Flommock grinned reassuringly. "My lips are sealed."

"Well, at the zoo today, I met a really nice kid from Africa. I gave him some of the quarters I got from the video arcade."

"What was he doing at the zoo when it was closed, son?"

"He works for Reggie," Little Max revealed. "And he told me that Reggie is not a geezer."

"An African boy working for a retired zookeeper? I don't think so, son."

"I know so, dad. His name is Pete and he came to America on the ship with the new animals. He helped Reggie put out the fire at the video arcade last night."

Flommock's eyes became squinty. "He did? That's strange. Hmmmm."

## Chapter Fourteen

On Saturday morning, more than two hundred people came to the zoo to see the new African animals. Reggie and Abby Sweet watched them arrive. In the distance, outside the gates, a dozen police cars and a fire truck supervised by Police Chief Grant Buxton sat like a herd of transformer machines.

The Devilish Duo arrived with their friends Cory, Jaime, Melly, LaToya, and Scooter. They could hardly wait until 3:00 p.m. for their bowling match, which Little Max had invited Peter to join. It would be a busy day at the bowling alley because the Women's Auxiliary Bowling Team, led by Holly Buxton and Libby Throttlebottom, wives of the Chief of Police and Mayor, also had their own semi-final tournament at noon.

Peter found Little Max and Bobby with their friends at the bowling alley's snack shop, waiting for their turn to bowl.

"Pete here knows everything there is to know about the new animals, doncha, Pete?" Little Max bragged.

"Well, certainly not everything," Peter corrected.

"Can you introduce us to them?" Melly Belloso asked.

"Yes, please, please, please," echoed Cory Chang and LaToya Tricklebank.

"I'd be happy to," Peter agreed. "Follow me!"

The children, led by Peter, strolled together towards the animals' cages.

As they passed the pool, they waved at The Scout Troop members, dressed in their water polo gear, looking forward to a game in the swimming pool. The pool had been refilled after Reggie and Peter had used much of its water to put out the arcade fire.

Reggie waved a cheery hello to members of the Senior Citizens Harley Davidson Motorcycle Club and residents of the Bedside Manor Retirement Home, including Tiny Teeny and Sadie. The two women were both happy they had something different to do that day, a departure from their usual routine of meals, card games, and TV. "I can't wait to see an Okapi!" Sadie sang, slipping a dried apricot into her mouth. "I'm in a Rhino mood myself," Tiny Teeny trilled, as her false teeth chattered.

Reggie smiled at a group of Japanese businessmen that came to visit the toy store to consider the purchase of substantial amounts of Ralph Bears, Wombats, and other Throttlebottom Toys for export to Japan.

He looked around for Bernie Moon but didn't see him in the crowd. He was disappointed, because the reporter had not returned his telephone call.

Nor did he find Edward Eugene Pincus from ICE, the Immigration and Naturalization Service, lurking around the gates,
observing everyone who entered the zoo. Pincus was the number one catcher of undocumented immigrants in America. Strapped to the belt around his waist, he wore a curved dagger with a Rhino horn handle. The man was so thin, he sometimes seemed to disappear.

Mayor Throttlebottom and his lackeys, Flommock, Winkleman, and Plitt, met at the gates and shook hands with Chief Buxton. They walked up the drive past the swimming pool where the Scouts were starting their water polo game and headed towards the main square. Throttlebottom saw the Japanese businessmen entering his toy store and he smiled happily, dollar signs dancing in his eyes.

Someone had forgotten to turn on the suction device that caused water from the fountain to pour out of Ralph Bear's mouth, so Throttlebottom reached down and turned on the spigot himself. As the water shot out of the Bear's mouth, a piece of red wood bounced on the ground in front of him. He picked it up and looked at it closely.

"What have you got there, Ralph?" Plitt asked.

"I dunno," he answered. "It sorta looks like a shingle from our office building roof."

Another piece of red wood fell from the skies and hit Plitt right on his bald head. "Ouch, that hurt!" he whined.

Three more slats sailed out, one of them skimming right past Flommock's ear, another hitting Winkleman on the shoulder.

"What's going on?" Throttlebottom cried. Then he looked up and spotted something that made him yell, "RUN!" They followed him as he scurried behind the Ralph Bear fountain for protection.

On top of the office building, Fingers, the Pygmy Chimpanzee, hurled a tree branch at them while Dirk, the Yellow Baboon, threw another wooden shingle. Emala, the Lowland Gorilla, beat her chest and roared as she stomped up and down on the flimsy roof.

"Ralph, what'll we do, Ralph?" cried Flommock.

"I left home without my cellphone," the mayor mumbled.

"Mine has run out of juice," Plitt hissed.

"I can't afford one!" Flommock cried.

"Let's make a run for the office building on the count of three," Throttlebottom demanded.

"Wait, Ralph!" Winkleman yelled. Wouldn't it be better to dash back to the gates and find Chief Buxton?"

"No, you idiot. It's faster to telephone 911 and the nearest phone is in the office. One...two...three!"

As the men hurried towards the building, Dirk and Fingers pulled more shingles from the roof and hurled them like Frisbees. Just as the men reached the entrance, Emala swung down from the roof, right to the doorway, blocking the door. She beat her chest and yowled.

## The Lincoln Zoo Rebellion

"He's going to kill us!" shouted Plitt, who seemed to think that all Gorillas were male. The men spun around and raced back to hide behind the fountain again.

Emala shrugged her shoulders and climbed back on the roof. *Reggie is right*, she told herself. *Those human animals sure are scared of us peaceful Gorillas.*

"Okay, Flommock," Throttlebottom cried. "You run down to the gates and bring back Buxton and the cops. Tell them to bring their guns! Plitt, you go to the bowling alley and tell my wife and all those bowling women to leave the zoo immediately. Go over to the toy store and tell those Tokyo businessmen to come back in a few days. Winkleman, you hurry over to the snack shops and merry-go-round and send everyone home."

Then Throttlebottom remembered there was a telephone in the veterinary surgery clinic, which was closer. He bounded towards it, his hands over his head fending off another barrage of shingles. He burst into the building and slammed the door behind him. Abby Sweet looked up from her desk.

"May I help you, sir?"

"Don't sweet talk me, Ms. Sweet," the Mayor warned. "There are three Apes on the office building roof, and I want to know how they got there. Did that nut case of a retired zookeeper let them out of their cages? Did you? I want some answers right now!"

"Reggie would never do such a thing, nor would I, Mr. Mayor," she said, "But I had better go find him. Those animals could hurt themselves up there."

"Those animals are threatening my life down here," Throttlebottom insisted. "Shoot them with tranquilizer darts."

"That's too dangerous, sir. They could fall off the roof! I'll locate Reggie and he will talk them down."

"Talk them down? Have you gone berserk too, Sweet?" Throttlebottom picked up the phone and dialed 911 for the police.

Abby Sweet rushed outside and glanced up to the office building roof. Sure enough, Dirk, Fingers, and Emala were *still* there, resting, and basking in the summer sun. At that moment, several of the Japanese businessmen were coming out of the toy store, which was a very bad idea. She shouted to them—in Japanese—to go back inside and stay there. She had learned to speak Japanese at University and was fluent in the language. They immediately spun around and went back into the store.

Abby ran as fast as her little legs would carry her to Reggie's cottage and called from the garden, "Reggie, come quick! The mayor thinks we let the Primates out!"

Reggie opened the door. "This is extremely serious," he said. "I thought I had the Chimp's agreement not to leave his cage until after dark, and I never even realized that the cages of Dirk and Emala were faulty, too. Follow me!"

He and Abby Sweet ran towards the square.

Black and white police cars sped past the gates and screeched to a halt in the square. Blue-uniformed bodies piled out of the cars. Some of them carried high-powered rifles with telescopic sights. Led by Police Chief Grant Buxton, they crawled on their stomachs from their cars to the fountain.

"Buxton!" Throttlebottom called from the veterinary surgery. "Cover me!"

Chief Buxton yelled, "Lock and load!" CLICKETY CLACK! The sound of six rifles being cocked made their point. "Aim!" All six rifles now pointed at the Primates on the roof. Throttlebottom waddled as fast as he could to the fountain.

Abby Sweet rushed up to the police. "Don't shoot, don't shoot!" cried the vet. "Reggie will persuade them to come down peacefully and go back to their cages."

"Hold your fire, men!" Chief Buxton ordered and sent the remaining policemen to drive their police cars to collect any remaining customers and safely remove them from the grounds of the zoo.

Reggie crawled along the rafters and through the attic window and onto the roof. He gestured to Fingers in Chimpanzee sign language and talked to Dirk at the same time in Baboon.

"What is that lunatic doing?" Throttlebottom screamed. "Shoot them, shoot them!"

"No, no," cried Abby Sweet, trying to force several policemen to put down their rifles. Chief Buxton ran over, picked her up and snatched her out of the line of fire. She kicked and yelled at him. "Put me down!"

"Look out!" cried a young policeman, standing up and raising his rifle to his shoulder. "That Gorilla is choking Reggie!"

"Wait! cried Abby Sweet. "She is only putting her arm around him!"

The rifle exploded.

Everyone froze.

Emala clutched her shoulder, her eyes bulging. Reggie looked up, stunned. The Gorilla took a step backward, crashed through the broken rafters, fell ten feet into Throttlebottom's office, bounced off his desk and landed unconscious on his couch in a shower of falling plaster.

"Oh no!" Abby Sweet howled. "This isn't happening!" She struggled out of Chief Buxton's grip and ran to the Veterinary Surgery room to find a stretcher. She emerged from the facility dragging a heavy stretcher on wheels along the newly laid, smooth tiles of the plaza and almost ran into six of the businessmen blocking her way. Their curiosity had made them brave enough to leave the store and look around. Abby implored them to follow her and help move the stretcher.

At the office building, Reggie and Peter removed fallen plaster from Emala's fur. Abby Sweet directed the businessmen to lift the Gorilla onto the stretcher and, as they pushed her to the surgery room, the vet clasped a towel to stop the bleeding from Emala's shoulder wound.

They took the unconscious Gorilla directly into the operating room, where Abby Sweet removed the blood-soaked towel and applied a thick, sterile gauze pad to help stop bleeding. She instructed the men to strap the Gorilla's arms and legs to the table as she gathered equipment for the operation.

"Here we go," she said slipping on her surgical mask and quickly washing her hands, then putting on rubber gloves. Emala lay unconscious the entire time.

Abby Sweet gave Emala a shot of anesthesia to make sure she didn't wake up and become excited or confused enough to hurt herself or others. Then she injected a few shots of lidocaine into the shoulder to make it numb. She needed to check for concussion, so she pulled open Emalas eyelids and shined a light on her pupils, to see if they had any sympathetic response. The pupils got smaller and larger as she passed the light over them, which told her that there was no brain damage. That was a relief. Abby then proceeded to insert a smooth tube called an "airway" into Emala's mouth, which insured that the Gorilla could take in enough air to breathe effortlessly.

She ordered one of the men to take Emala's blood pressure every five minutes. Then she shaved the thick hair off the area of the wound and began cleaning it. She flushed the wound with saline, which is a sort of salty sterilized water. When that was finished, she packed the wound with gauze, and bathed the area around the wound with tincture of green soap. Finally, she proceeded to sew it up with silk sutures.

Reggie called softly from the back of the room, "I hate to be nosy, Abby Sweet, but if you are already sewing up the wound, what about the bullet inside her? Don't you need to extract it?"

"No," she replied. "First I must close the wound. Then I will take X-rays to see if the bullet requires immediate extraction. If it is not in a dangerous spot, I'll allow Emala to recover from her state of shock for several weeks before removing it."

Dirk and Fingers swung into the room and joined Reggie, quietly observing the operation.

After sewing up the wound, Abby Sweet created a full shoulder bandage, gave Emala a shot of antibiotic, and double-checked Emala's blood pressure yet again. It was stable, though her pulse was still weak. One of the businessmen informed her that he knew how to operate the digital X-ray machine and she gave him the go ahead.

The entire treatment had taken thirty minutes, after which Abbey Sweet plopped down on a stool, exhausted.

Five minutes later, the businessman on the x-ray machine brought up an X-ray picture on the computer of Emala's shoulder. "There's the bullet," Abby Sweet said, pointing. "It's lodged in the muscle towards her left shoulder blade. Not a dangerous spot. It won't do any harm to leave it inside her for a couple of weeks. It's over."

"I'm afraid it has just begun," warned Reggie. "Our enemies have fired the first shot, and we must confront them. Fingers! Dirk! Come with me! We will present our demands to the Board, and we must make them listen."

"But Reggie," Abby Sweet pleaded. "In order to persuade them you are going to have to tell them your secret talent—that you can *actually* speak to the animals."

"You are right, my dear. But I think it is the only way forward."

Arm-in-arm, Reggie, Fingers and Dirk marched out of the surgery.

The Board meeting was almost finished. Throttlebottom had revealed his new plans for rebuilding the zoo. His wife's nephew had raved about a new waterpark in the Catskill Mountains that had Flowrider surfing, a laser tag adventure game, virtual reality white water rafting, and a gamer's paradise video arcade far bigger than the one that Blomm the Elephant destroyed. He asked for a vote of approval.

"But that would take up a lot of space, Ralph," said Flommock. What about the animals, Ralph?"

The mayor pondered the question. "I suggest we offer them to the Lincoln Park Zoo in Chicago. Every once in a while, they could bring the biggest animals to our water park in glass cages and the kids could look at them as they hurdle down the water tube slides."

"Any objections?" Throttlebottom banged his gavel three times. "Passed, passed, passed! All motions are hereby carried and passed!"

## The Lincoln Zoo Rebellion

Just then, Reggie and the Primates appeared at the doorway to the conference room. Chief Buxton drew his pistol and pointed it at Dirk. "I've got 'em covered."

"Drop your gun, Buxton," demanded Reggie. "These animals will not harm anyone, and we don't want another senseless accident, do we?" Reggie's serious eyes sent a message. Buxton lowered his gun, but still kept it on the table.

Reggie continued calmly. "First of all, gentlemen, Emala the Gorilla's condition is stable for the time being, thanks to the brilliant surgery by Abby Sweet."

"Maybe we should reconsider and not fire her," Winkleman whispered to Throttlebottom.

"Shut up, you fool! He can hear everything," replied the mayor.

"So, you have decided to fire one of the best veterinary surgeons I have ever seen, have you?" said Reggie, shaking his head in dismay. "This is one more example of your gross stupidity and mismanagement. We will not tolerate this any longer. Here is a list of demands from me and all the animals in this zoo."

Reggie pulled out the twenty-page roll of paper from his overalls and placed it on the table. "Everything on this list is practical and affordable. The animals are to be given first priority at this zoo. They are the stars here and stars deserve star treatment."

"Yeah, yeah, yeah," interrupted Throttlebottom. "I've heard all this prattle before. We reject it, Pops. We've just voted to rebuild the video arcade and add a fantastic water park. And we don't want habitats, whatever they are, or animal mates or any other thing on that paper of yours."

Reggie rose to his full height, which was taller than expected. "We are not making a request, gentlemen. This is a demand. The animals are with me one hundred percent, from Aardvark to Elephant, from Lion to Rhino, from Tiger to Wildebeest."

"That's a laugh!" Throttlebottom exclaimed. "Can you believe this guy?" he said to Buxton and the others. "I told you he was off his rocker."

"I speak their languages," Reggie admitted calmly, "and together we have the power to force you to agree."

"Aw, come on," chuckled Winkleman. "That's ridiculous. You can't talk to animals. No one can! You're no Doctor Doolittle. That's a fictional character."

"I knew you would mock me, and that is why I have brought Dirk and Fingers here to prove my abilities. Think of any impossible task you wish them to perform and I will tell them in their own language to do it."

Flommock stammered, "Gee, Reggie, I don't know, Reggie. Well, ask the Baboon to turn a somersault, toss me my hat, and climb up on and off the chair four times."

Plitt laughed. "Yeah. And tell that other Monkey to go jump in the lake. Ha, ha, ha," he chuckled with delight.

Reggie translated for Dirk and Fingers, using grunts and clicks of the Baboon and Chimp languages. Dirk somersaulted over to the hat stand, tossed the zoo president his hat and climbed up and down on the chair four times.

Fingers had a problem about jumping into water. He mind-talked to Reggie that Chimps can't swim very well because their low body fat ratio causes them to sink and it's difficult to keep their heads above water. Reggie explained this to the men in English and asked them to come up with another task for Fingers. Besides, Veronica Lake was a long way away.

"That's ridiculous," said Winkleman.

"You're right. What is the point of all this?" Throttlebottom cried. "You are wasting our time!"

"If you think the rights of the animals are a waste of time, then you should spend some time in a cage yourself and see what *that* is like," Reggie answered angrily. He continued:

"You will be stunned to learn that because you skimped on the quality of building materials, the new cages are faulty. One word from me and the animals will break out of those cheap, flimsy cages and storm the zoo! Approve our demands today or you will have a revolution on your hands. A full-scale rebellion!"

"I don't think we will, old man," sneered Throttlebottom. Then he made a terrifying threat. "At this very moment, twenty-seven sharpshooters with high-powered rifles are stationed in front of the cages. If any animal so much as rattles a bar, they have orders to shoot to kill. Chief Buxton will change the guards every eight hours around the clock until Calhoun gets here to fix the cages or bring brand new ones.

"We will allow Abby Sweet to stay on the premises until the Gorilla recovers and then she's fired for gross insubordination. And furthermore, I have recently learned from Mr. Flommock here that you have personally been concealing an illegal alien boy named Pete at this zoo. He is being tracked by Edward Eugene Pincus of ICE, the immigration people, and the moment he catches the kid he will be deported to Africa on the first plane out and you will go to jail. That's it, and that's all!"

Reggie boiled. His face turned red and he felt as if smoke was coming out of his ears. He took a deep breath and yelled at the top of his lungs, "Ahhkecccht okk. Ahhkecccht okkee," the traditional Gorilla warning, hoping Peter could hear it.

Then he closed his eyes tightly and beamed his most powerful mind-projection to all animals warning them about the sharpshooters. Many of the animals understood and explained it to the animals that didn't understand Reggie. After a short pause, the zoo population of animals responded with roaring, braying, screeching, howling, and the most awful caterwauling ever before heard in one place. That was spine tingling scary!

Reggie took a deep breath. "That, gentlemen, was the unified vote of the animals telling you they shall overcome. But I need to do my part. I am going on a hunger strike. From this moment on I shall not eat or drink until you agree to our demands. If they are not met, you will have the blood of an old zookeeper on your consciences forever. And the public may not be so pleasant about it."

Reggie thrust his right fist in the air, thumb pointing at the tip of his nose and pinkie finger extended towards the zoo directors in a Mountain Gorilla power salute. He stormed out of the room, Dirk and Fingers following.

Peter heard Reggie's call from inside the bowling alley where he was enjoying his game with Little Max, Bobby and the other children. He put down his heavy bowling ball. "I'm sorry guys, but I must stop playing immediately. Reggie has gone on a hunger strike and my life is in danger. I have to leave the zoo immediately. We should all go together. Something is terribly wrong. Can anyone help me get away from the zoo quickly?"

"I can!" cried Scooter Goldfarb, whose real name was Melvin. "Hop on my new scooter and I'll get you out of here lickety-split!"

## Chapter Fifteen

"It's dangerous for a man your age to be on a hunger strike," warned Abby Sweet. "At least let me give you some vitamin supplements."

"No, my dear," Reggie sighed. "I shall fast until the rebellion is finished and we have won. Don't worry, Abby Sweet. I'm stronger than you think."

This was the third day of Reggie's hunger strike and conditions remained the same. Teams of sharpshooters guarded all the cages around the clock and Reggie beamed words of caution to the animals on a regular basis.

No message was received from Peter, who had successfully disappeared. With instructions from Pincus of ICE, Chief Buxton had put out an all-points bulletin for the arrest of Peter.

There were several reports of Peter sightings, especially in the hills North of Lincoln called Horace Heights and Clint East Woods, but none of them checked out to be Peter. Someone living next to Lincoln Hills Middle School called the police at midnight to complain about the annoying sound of tennis balls being hit against the wall, but when the police cars arrived, no one was there.

Emala regained consciousness and continued to make progress under Abby Sweet's care. The Gorilla found it hard to focus her eyes and was constantly dizzy, making Abby Sweet more concerned that she might have a minor concussion from her fall through the roof.

Strangely enough, nothing about the Primates' escape from their cages, or even Emala's shooting was printed in the *Lincoln Examiner.* The paper did, however, publish a front-page picture of Throttlebottom, proclaiming that the new zoo is open for business as usual, and that everyone should ignore any fake rumors they may hear about any troubles there. He offered free toys for every admission and free soft drinks. He also mentioned that the local police staff were on a training mission at the zoo and that patrons should not be concerned that anything was amiss.

"Are you sure this is a good idea to keep the zoo open during these troubled times?" Winkleman asked.

"Don't be stupid," Throttlebottom answered. "We've got a business to run. You can't just close down money-making properties on a whim!"

"But we might be putting people in danger," Flommock whimpered.

"Business is business, Max! "The zoo is open!" Throttlebottom barked. "And that's the way it is!"

There were no gardening stories by Bernie Moon in the *Tribune* either. Reggie called the reporter two or three times to make contact with him, but to no avail.

"This is serious," Reggie told Abby Sweet. "If we can't obtain any publicity, my hunger strike will have no effect whatsoever. If the people of Lincoln don't even know I am starving to death, they won't do anything to help us."

"Then stop your fast!" Abby Sweet said firmly. But Reggie would not.

He tried to phone other reporters on the *Examiner*, to ask them to write about his hunger strike, but when they heard it was him on the line, they would usually just hang up. "Sorry, Reggie," one of them said. "My editor is not allowed to print any zoo news until further notice."

In the afternoon of the third day, Little Max Flommock insisted that his father drive him to the zoo to see Reggie. He brought a cardboard box with him, to carry the big bowl of mushroom soup that he had cooked all by himself. Flommock was impressed that his son was so thoughtful, but he didn't want to confront the zookeeper, so he waited for Bobby in the limo outside the gates while the boy delivered the soup.

Little Max and Reggie chatted on the front doorstep of the cottage. Reggie, of course, refused to drink the soup, but he was surprised and pleased by Little Max's gesture. "I will keep it in my refrigerator for when the rebellion is over, and the animals have won their rights...and my hunger strike ends."

"Okay," Little Max whispered. "I have something to tell you. At the bowling alley, my friends and I listened to Pete talk about animals and their feelings and stuff. He made us think about them in a different way, and we're sorry we've been rude to them."

"Goodness Greyhounds!" Reggie said, surprised. "Did I hear you say, 'my friends and I,' and not 'me and my friends?'"

"Yeah," Little Max smirked. "I guess I'm learning good, okay?"

"I think you are learning very WELL indeed," Reggie beamed.

"Also, I'm very sorry I told my dad about Peter being here," Little Max apologized. "I told him it was a secret. I didn't think he would tell the mayor."

"I won't hold it against you," Reggie comforted Little Max. "I just wish I knew Peter was okay. I'm so concerned about him."

"Don't worry, Reggie. Peter is safe," he whispered. "We're taking care of him. My dad doesn't know."

"Wow!" Reggie was pleasantly surprised.

"Can I please have the cardboard box Pete stashed in your front closet with his clean T-shirts and spare tennis shoes and other stuff?" Little Max went on.

He then hurried back to the limo. When Big Max Flommock saw him carrying the cardboard box containing Peter's items, he assumed that it was the same box with the soup that his son cooked for the zookeeper. "He didn't take the soup, eh?"

"Nope," fibbed Little Max.

Driving down Belly Button Blvd, Flommock didn't notice the white car following him. It was Pincus of ICE, who had been hiding in the bushes next to Reggie's cottage. He had heard Little Max tell Reggie about helping Peter. The immigration investigator made a quick call to police headquarters from his cellphone and informed Chief Buxton that he was now on the trail of the fugitive African youth.

On the fourth day, Reggie stayed in bed. Abby Sweet, again, tried to persuade him to eat something, but he refused. Sadly, while Emala was becoming stronger and recovering an even pulse, Reggie's energy was steadily decreasing. He stayed up in his sleeping platform and tried to beam thoughts of good will to the animals, but his mind-projections were becoming weaker and weaker.

The animals became frightened and jittery about Reggie's condition. The Felines, including Milt the Tiger, Goliath, and Lady Gaga were especially anxious, since they relied on Reggie's reassuring messages more than the other animals did. They prowled around their cages in a state of high-strung tension. Goliath, who had known and loved the old zookeeper longest, wailed, ranted, and roared. The sharpshooter guarding him never removed his finger from the trigger of the rifle.

Abby Sweet sent e-mails to the board members, pleading with them to do something, anything, to solve the situation, but she received no response. She telephoned Bernie Moon several times, but the same recorded message repeated every time, and the machine would not take a message. She sent him an e-mail and several texts, as well.

Abby Sweet summoned Dr. McGillicuddy from the Bedside Manor Retirement Home and together they climbed the rickety steps of the sleeping platform.

Reggie was lying on his back, eyes shut, dressed in frilly white pajamas with navy blue piping. His arms were crossed on his chest, and he had a smile on his lips. The ends of his white mustache were unusually ragged. His bushy black eyebrows twitched…

"Dear, dear, dear," the doctor sighed. "I'm going to have to put him on intravenous feeding."

Reggie's eyes opened wide. "No, you're not, McGillicuddy! No soup in the mouth, no sugar in a tube in my arm!" Then he closed his eyes again.

"Now, now, my friend, no arguments," the doctor insisted. "I will organize a hospital bed for you tomorrow. The ambulance will arrive at one o'clock. Do you hear me?"

"Oh well," Reggie mumbled weakly. "Tomorrow will probably be the end."

The fifth day of Reggie's hunger strike began. A terrible sadness descended over Abby Sweet as she held Reggie's hand while he dozed on the sleeping platform. She had stayed with him all night, mopping his brow with a damp cloth, until dawn broke and the Birds around the zoo came alive with crowing and heavenly bird calls. Reggie heard Cosmo the Flamingo and Penguins calling for him…but it could have been in his dreams.

Everything was quiet, except for the scuffling of the police sharpshooters changing shifts in front of the animals' cages at dawn. The policeman who had taken over the assignment to guard Lady Gaga could hardly see straight. He had been up half the night due to his wife's loud snoring.

At 7:45 in the morning, Little Max Flommock boarded the Number 8 bus in front of his house and rode it past Lincoln Station to the Ankle Avenue stop.

He met Bobby Winkleman and a number of other children there. The group walked up the dirt path for about a mile until they came to Veronica Lake. Inside one of the shacks, which used to be a fishing tourist cabin, they greeted Peter, who had quietly been hiding out from Pincus. They gave him all the food they had pinched from their refrigerators at home and unpacked their boxes.

"This is by far the best hiding place," Little Max said. In the past few days, Little Max had hidden Peter out in different places: First, in the gym at the Barack Obama Middle School, where Peter had snuck out at midnight to hit tennis balls against the wall; then the men's bathroom at Plitt's gas station; and just a few days at a tool shed in Cory Chang's garden. The shack was by far the best hiding place.

Peter was pleased that the other children were interested in helping with the peaceful protest. At their various meetings, he had discussed the variety of protest methods they could use, including picketing where people congregate outside a particular business location, where they could hold signs and try to persuade people not to enter the premises.

"Perhaps we should get all our friends to picket the zoo until they improve the animals' situation," Peter suggested.

"Great idea, señor Pete," Jaime Gutierrez exclaimed. "I can get all the kids from my Sunday school class to do that."

"I'll call all my amigos and tell them we are boycotting the zoo!" Melly Belloso echoed. "Boy, will my parents be surprised. They complain I like to visit the zoo too often."

"Okay," Little Max ordered. "If we're going to picket, we need signs. Let's start painting!" The group scattered to find the sign-making materials.

At the same time, Flommock was on the phone with Throttlebottom, pleading with him to find a compromise. "Ralph, we are murdering that old geezer. He wouldn't even eat my kid's mushroom soup, Ralph."

The mayor wouldn't listen. "Don't bother me, Max. I've got to drive to the toy factory right away. Those Japanese businessmen are about to sign an order for six million Ralph Bears." He hung up.

At the Bedside Manor Retirement Home, Sadie and Tiny Teeny were arguing. "I counted twenty-one stripes up the legs of the Okapi," said Sadie, proudly. Tiny Teeny had counted only twenty. The great-grandmothers agreed to go to the zoo to recount the stripes and take a deck of playing cards for a game of gin rummy.

At 11:00 a.m., Winkleman and Plitt arrived at the zoo to supervise the builders who were hired to repair the roof of the office building and to take delivery of the brand-new cages from *Calhoun Critter Cages*.

"Let's get over to the conference room," Winkleman urged. "We don't want to miss the wrestling match finals on TV."

At the swimming pool, the boys from the Scout Troop were readying themselves for another challenging game of water polo. Their scoutmaster proudly introduced them to his new fiancée, a beautiful blonde woman with luminous blue eyes.

## The Lincoln Zoo Rebellion

At 11:30 a.m., the Women's Auxiliary Bowling Team arrived at the Bowling Alley. Today would be the finals of their year-long tournament. The mayor's wife, Libby Throttlebottom, led one of the teams, while Holly Buxton, wife of the Chief of Police, captained the opposing team. The women all gossiped for a long time before starting to bowl.

Close to noon, a pushcart vendor started his rounds at the zoo. It was his job to feed all the police sharpshooters and today was a special day for him. The night before, his wife had delivered an eleven-pound baby girl, so he decided to give each policeman a special treat: a double-size hotdog stuffed with cheese and dipped in chili, topped with his special tangy sauerkraut and hot Tabasco sweet pickles. Yum.

Meanwhile at Veronica Lake, the children emerged from the tourist cabin with the special artwork they had created: brightly painted signs and placards which read:

**ANIMALS HAVE RIGHTS**
**HEY YOU! DON'T RUIN MY ZOO**
**HABITATS NOT CAGES!**
**IF YOU DON'T WANT A WEDGIE, BRING BACK REGGIE**
**MAYOR UNFAIR**
**WE WANT REGGIE**

"It's time to start picketing," yelled Little Max.
"We're ready," Cory Chang and LaToya Tricklebank joined in.
"Let's go!" Peter boomed.
Suddenly, Officer Edward Eugene Pincus from ICE appeared in front of them, waving his Rhino horn dagger. "Stop right there!" he ordered. Everyone froze.

Pincus looked at them all, perplexed. "Which one of you is the illegal African alien, Peter Nelson N'gara?" There was silence for a moment. No one breathed.

"We all are!" Bobby Winkleman shouted. "Scatter, guys!"

Pincus didn't know which one to follow, as the children ran in all directions at once. Peter had dressed them in the costumes from the harvest festival of Mombasa. In the confusion, all Pincus saw was a banana, a mango, a bunch of grapes, a head of celery, a giant peach, and a huge carrot with carrot-top running about.

A large pineapple skipped nonchalantly down the path, wearing tennis shoes. Pincus ran right past it, chasing a giant kumquat on a scooter.

Back at the zoo, a bus carrying the Japanese trade delegates arrived. They had concluded their transactions at the toy factory and had several hours to kill before going to the airport to catch their plane home. They headed directly for the toy store.

Also, at that moment, an ambulance pulled out of the garage of Lincoln General Hospital, turned on its siren and headed for the zoo to pick up Reggie. The attendant in the back seat prepared the oxygen and emergency equipment.

At 12:30 p.m., the scoutmaster and his beautiful blonde fiancée bought tickets for the merry-go-round. "Don't you think you should check on the boys at the swimming pool, lovey pie?" the girl asked.

"Naw, they'll be okay, sweet lump. Let's have a ride first. "I'll take the polka-dot pony. You try the furry sheep."

Lady Gaga, the Leopard, watched her police sharpshooter guard through the bars of the cage. The hotdog he had for lunch sat like a lump in the sharpshooter's stomach and he couldn't stop yawning from his sleepless night. He curled up on the bench only to rest, after leaning the rifle against the bench. The Leopard watched him nod off to sleep, and the rifle slowly slipping to the ground. Convinced he was completely out of it, she took a bar of the cage in her teeth and quietly snapped it off. She removed another bar, and yet another, and slipped through to freedom. The policeman snored on.

The ambulance stopped in front of Reggie's cottage. The driver and attendant grabbed a stretcher and knocked on the door. Abby Sweet had been anxiously waiting for them, and quickly ran to the door and welcomed them in. They rushed up the rickety steps to the sleeping platform, rolled Reggie onto his side and strapped him securely to the stretcher.

The Lady Gaga heard the sound of the merry-go-round calliope playing "The Teddy Bear's Picnic." She advanced, stealthily, pressing her body as close to the ground as she could. She spotted a curvy shaped animal with a mane of golden hair slipping up and down, never wavering off course.

Suddenly, the natural senses of Lady Gaga made her forget she was in a zoo. Now, as a healthy, hungry Leopard, she was back in the bush and there, before her, moved some tasty looking game.

The scoutmaster and his fiancée rode merrily next to one another, oblivious to the danger. They leaned over and pressed their lips together in a tender, eyeball-to-eyeball kiss.

At that moment, the Leopard bounded down the path at 36 miles per hour, leaped in the air, and sank her teeth into the throat of the carousel sheep, inches from the scoutmaster's fiancée. It made an odd crunching sound.

The girl shrieked like a banshee and slipped to the floor. "Leaping Leopards!" shouted the scoutmaster, sliding off the pony, picking his girlfriend up and jumping to the ground. The operator of the machinery, the ticket collector, and all the customers ran for their lives.

"Ptooey!" spat the Leopard, when she realized she was biting into paper mache and sawdust instead of a raw, living lamb chop. She was so angry, she began to demolish the cute little merry-go-round animals one by one. Without the operator to run the merry-go-round, the machine picked up speed. "The Teddy Bear's Picnic" ran faster and faster and faster as steam hissed through the calliope, forcing ear-shattering whistles and dreadful discords into the air.

The police sharpshooters around the zoo heard the crazy speeding-up merry-go-round music and shouts of "Help!" from the customers. They left their posts at the defective animal cages and came running, rifles at the ready.

The animals, seeing the armed sharpshooters leaving their posts, attacked the bars of their cages with ferocity and vigor. Blomm ripped his leg shackles right off the tree stumps that were holding them and careered towards the Ralph Bear fountain. The Black Rhino crashed through his bars and thundered past the swimming pool. He and Blomm pulled up short before they ran into each other in the square.

Rambo, the ancient Hippo, couldn't free himself from his older, better-built cage, so Blomm and the Black Rhino cooperatively smashed into it, lifting up the entire frame, allowing Rambo to squeeze out underneath.

The three of them attacked other cages with brute strength. They freed Sigmund Crocodile and Adolf Alligator easily. Then

## The Lincoln Zoo Rebellion

the Hyena, who wasn't as bulky as the others, but had the most powerful jaws of any animal at the zoo, helped them liberate Milt the Tiger, Sam the Giraffe, Lyle the Lynx, the Cheetah, and all the other caged creatures. Blomm and the Black Rhino ran back through the square, the ground reverberating under their trampling feet.

"What's that?" asked the attendant holding the end of the stretcher with Reggie's feet.

"It sounds like an earthquake," the driver added, holding the front end with Reggie's head. "Did you hear something, Miss?" they asked Abby Sweet.

"No! please hurry!" she cried.

The attendant stepped down one more step, which was one step too many. It cracked, shattered, and gave way, causing the stretcher—with Reggie strapped to it—to sail over his head, bounce down the rest of the steps, skid along the floor, and crash into the front door.

Abby Sweet's eyes opened wide with horror. "Are you alright, Reggie?" she cried out?

With the stretcher still strapped to his back, Reggie jumped to his feet, looking like a man strapped to a boat sail. He turned and looked up at Abby Sweet, then at the startled ambulance men, and a wide smile came to his face. His eyes sparkled brightly.

"Get me out of this thing!" he shouted with glee. "They're free! The animals have escaped their cages! So have all the birds—even Cosmo the Flamingo and those silly Penguins. The rebellion has begun!"

## Chapter Sixteen

Reggie threw off the restraints of the stretcher, opened the front door, sniffed the air, and cocked his ears to see if he could perceive any animal mind-messages in the air. He marched proud and tall, taking giant strides as if he were a general entering a battlefield. The fact he had not eaten in days and had lost several pounds didn't faze him one bit.

Abby Sweet rushed to keep up with him. "Where did all the police guards go?" Reggie called to the Wildebeest as it gamboled by. She paused and informed him with her nasal 'meeark' sounds about the calamity at the merry-go-round.

Dirk rushed up to Reggie. "There are a bunch of middle-aged ladies bowling in the alley," declared the Baboon, "and the Penguins have followed them inside. Two old ladies are playing cards in front of the Okapi, two zoo directors are hiding inside the office building, several hairy men are fixing the roof, and a bunch of kids are throwing a ball around in the swimming pool."

"Right!" Reggie lit up at the news. "We've got to find a way to move those riflemen from the merry-go-round into the bowling alley. I've got an idea."

The merry-go-round gyrated wildly out of control with Lady Gaga hanging on for dear life. The policemen dodged hunks of paper maché ponies and flying sawdust as the carousel animals broke up from the powerful spinning force. The captain ordered his men to kill the Leopard. "Fire!" he yelled. But Lady Gaga was an elusive blur because the machine was spinning too fast for them to take proper aim.

Reggie and Abby Sweet dashed up to the police captain. "Help! Help!" they both cried. "It's the Women's Auxiliary! They're trapped in the bowling alley. The Elephant has escaped again. So has the Black Rhino, and the mayor's wife is in there!"

"Oh, no!" the captain cried. "Not Mrs. Throttlebottom!"

"Yes!" Abby Sweet reinforced, "And so is Holly Buxton, the wife of your Chief of Police! The Crocodile is after her! Hurry!"

"Follow me, men!" the captain ordered, and all the policemen took off, racing towards the bowling alley to save the lives of the women, whose husbands controlled their salaries, bonuses, and pensions.

Reggie turned to Abby Sweet. "The *Crocodile* is after her? He's so overweight, he couldn't catch her if she was crawling!"

"It sure moved those policemen!" Abby Sweet smiled.

Bill Winkleman and Howard Plitt sat in the conference room of the office building, watching a wrestling match on a portable TV, oblivious to the commotion going on outside. It was a little hard for them to hear the commotion of the rebellion with the workmen busy hammering new wooden shingles onto the roof above them.

Suddenly, the hammering stopped and one of the men yelled down from the roof, "Hey, we'll come back and finish this job another time. You got a bunch of loose animals running wild out here!"

"Huh?" Plitt turned down the TV and ran to the window just in time to see Milt the Tiger running past at forty miles-per-hour, being easily passed by the fastest animal in the world, the Cheetah, a blur at seventy-miles-per-hour. Plitt leaned out the window in disbelief when suddenly the Spotted Hyena, which had been hiding in the bushes, jumped up in front of his face and laughed his frenzied cackle, scaring the secretary-treasurer half to death.

"Get the mayor on the phone," he shrieked at Winkleman, who frantically grabbed his smart phone and punched in the toy factory number.

"Where are all the police sharpshooters?" Winkleman asked.

"There they are!" said Plitt looking out the window. "They're running towards the bowling alley!"

"Why would they go bowling at a time like this?" Winkleman stammered as he waited for someone to answer the phone.

Reggie mind-projected to Blomm to barricade the doors of the bowling alley. The Elephant quite agreeably did exactly as he was told. He uprooted the stumps of two large trees and dumped them in front of the doors. He then stood guard. "There is no way anyone will leave this building as long as Blomm is on duty," he trumpeted to the universe.

Reggie pulled the electrical fuse for the merry-go-round, causing the out-of-control ride to slow down in a long, screeching, grinding, shower of sparks, halt. Lady Gaga, her sharp claws dug deep into the paper maché of a carousel pony to keep from being thrown off the spinning machine, tried to catch her breath and waited for her dizzy world to come into focus.

"Thanks!" she called out in Leopard.

"Now we must clear the zoo, as best we can, before somebody gets hurt," Reggie told Abby Sweet. "This rebellion must be nonviolent!"

"You call this non-violent?" she asked, surprised.

"It's certainly energetic," Reggie corrected himself. "But yes. So far, I think it's non-violent. Well…maybe a teeny bit violent."

"I'll try to move the people safely out of the toy store," she answered. Do you have the strength to see to the scouts?"

"You bet," he smiled, heading towards the swimming pool. After a brisk run, he came upon the scoutmaster and his blue-eyed fiancée, who was laid out on a park bench in a dead faint. "Pick her up and follow me," Reggie ordered. "You boys and girls have to leave this zoo immediately!"

The scouts were noisily playing a frenzied game of water polo in the shallow end as the scoutmaster yelled, "Get outa the pool!" But they couldn't hear him. Suddenly, a huge blob of grey blubber cannonballed into the pool, creating an enormous tidal wave that engulfed the surprised polo players.

When the tsunami subsided, the scouts coughed up water, cleared their eyes, and looked to the deep end to see a huge Hippopotamus, joyfully paddling in place. The kids flew out of the pool and ran. Rambo snorted and sank happily to the bottom.

Reggie safely escorted the dripping scouts and their perspiring scoutmaster, with his blonde fiancée thrown over his shoulders, to the zoo entrance. He closed the gates behind them. Goliath came over to see how Reggie was feeling. Reggie assured his old friend that he was okay and asked the Lion to stand at the ticket booth and not let anyone enter the zoo without his permission. Goliath nodded and bounded off.

Abby Sweet looked in the window of the toy store, but there was no danger. She saw nothing but happiness, with Fingers playing with an electronic football game, Durante watching a toy electric train spinning around a track, Spider Monkeys swinging from the rafters, and Louie the Lemur entertaining his new girlfriend—a Barbie Doll. Huddled together in a corner, the toy store employees and the Japanese trade delegates looked like one frightened family. Abby motioned them to follow her.

She quickly led them to the gates, then waved good-bye to the Japanese businessmen and thanked them again for their help with Emala's operation. At the ticket booth, Goliath roared a loud "Goodbye" as they hurried off, running to find their van in the parking lot.

"Throttlebottom Toy Factory, home of the famous Ralph Bear," the lilting voice of the receptionist answered the phone at Winkleman.

"What took you so long?" roared vice-president Winkleman. "Get me Throttlebottom instantly."

"Sorry, sir, the mayor is in conference."

"Get him out of conference right now and tell him the animals here, at the zoo, are about to eat his wife!"

"Hold please," the secretary cooed.

Throttlebottom picked up the phone. 'What do you want, I'm busy."

"He's done it, Ralph."

"Who?"

"Reggie!"

"That ex-zookeeper geezer? I thought he was dead." Throttlebottom retorted.

"Not yet, but he did do it." Winkleman gasped.

"Do what? Spit it out, Bill."

"He let, he let loose, you know, he really..." Winkleman stuttered.

"Gimme Plitt! I can't understand a word you're saying!" Throttlebottom barked.

Winkleman thrust the phone at secretary-treasurer Plitt. "*You* tell him."

"The animals are running amok and your wife is here." Plitt wheezed.

"Where?"

"Here at the zoo, where else?" Plitt sounded annoyed.

"Where are the police sharpshooters?"

"In the bowling alley with your wife."

"Bowling? Where's Buxton?" Throttlebottom pressed.

"MIA – Missing in action."

"So where are the animals?"

## The Lincoln Zoo Rebellion

"Everywhere!" Plitt raised his voice. "Try to concentrate, Ralph. Every beast in this zoo is running around loose. 'Loose,' as in unfettered, unchained, unshackled, unbound, and uncaged. 'Loose," as in about to attack and kill us all because of that hunger-striking old Goat."

"I'll be there in a flash," Throttlebottom blurted out, dropping the receiver. He then barged out of his office, his face beet-red and his eyes bulging. He ran down the assembly line of toy animal stuffers, hollering instructions to his secretary. "Call Flommock! Get my limo!"

The poor woman ran behind him. "He can't afford a cellphone, Mr. Mayor! So I can't reach him. You'll have to drive yourself." The mayor changed direction and headed for the garage entrance, yelling, "Cancel my appointments! Send ambulances to the zoo! Alert the hospital!"

A heavily made-up woman with curly black hair, who had been stuffing a Willy Wombat on the assembly line, jumped into the mayor's path. "What happened?" she cried.

"Outa my way," yelled the mayor pushing her aside. "The animals at the zoo are loose." He ran to the garage entrance.

The Willy Wombat stuffer threw down her unfinished toy, grabbed a backpack from under her desk and headed in the opposite direction toward the main exit. She pushed through the revolving door and stumbled out onto the pavement. Feeling a cold sensation on her scalp, she grabbed her head. It was bald! She turned her head around and saw a mass of black curls stuck in the door. Oh, no! Her wig!

She whistled for a taxi but there was none in sight. Then she spied a long maroon Cadillac limousine stopped at a red light and ran up to its driver. "Can you take me to Lincoln Zoo for ten bucks?"

"S...s...sure," stuttered Flommock, putting on his official-looking cap. "Hop in." The limo pulled away from the light and the woman suddenly realized who the driver was. "Flommock, is that you?" she asked.

Big Max Flommock looked in the rear-view mirror. "Yeah, but who are you?"

"It's me, Bernie Moon!" He immediately tugged and pulled off the rubber cap that made his head look bald, and worked feverishly to wipe off the lipstick and rouge that made him look like a woman. "I've been pretending to be a Willy Wombat stuffer for an article about pollution and crimes against the environment and global warming right here at the toy factory."

"Who's gonna print it, Moon? The *Examiner* won't publish anything you write." Flommock questioned.

Bernie Moon laughed, as he pulled off his false eyelashes. "I've got a new job on the *Chicago Tribune*! They loved my story about man-eating plants. But now there's an even hotter story at the zoo, so step on it!"

"What's happening at the zoo?" Flommock exclaimed.

"All the animals are loose!"

"Oh no!" Flommock floored the limo as he sped past Plitt's garage on Nostril Way, past his own wrecked used car lot with the Steals 'n Deals sign lying flat on the ground. Then Bernie Moon spotted a small procession of walking fruit on the shoulder of the road ahead, led by a pineapple. "What the heck is that?"

"I think it's a bunch of kids dressed up as fruit and vegetables, Moon," Flommock said, sarcastically.

## The Lincoln Zoo Rebellion

"Cute," said the reporter, as he pulled out his camera from the backpack and fired off a few photos.

Bernie Moon then pulled out his cellphone and punched in the number for the TV station. He told them to send a camera crew out to the zoo on the double. "Save me three minutes on the six o'clock news!" he exclaimed, "I've got an exclusive!"

Milt the Tiger and the Cheetah, out of breath from running around in the zoo, joined Reggie as he checked out the current situation. As they passed Reggie's cottage, Reggie saw his friends, Sadie and Tiny Teeny, knocking on his front door.

"Hey, there!" Reggie hailed them.

"Oh Reggie!" Tiny Teeny brightened. "We were playing gin rummy and counting the Okapi's stripes when suddenly he was out of his cage, twisting and twirling down the path, ripping out tiger lilies."

"I know," reassured Reggie. "It's nothing for you to be troubled about, good ladies. Sometimes a few beautiful flowers must be sacrificed in the name of history. You are eyewitnesses to the first zoo animals' rebellion ever!"

"That sounds quite exciting, dear," said Tiny Teeny dryly. "But how about a cup of your peppermint tea? That would be even more exciting right now."

"Help yourselves to tea and snickerdoodles," Reggie said, expansively opening the door for them. "And please stay here in the cottage until things calm down a bit."

Police Chief Grant Buxton's cellphone rang. "I'm sorry," he apologized to four poker playing buddies who were gambling at a secret house on Meryl Streep Street. "I'd better answer it." He put the phone up to his ear. "Hello?"

"Where the blazes are you Buxton?" demanded the mayor. "I'm in my yellow limo driving to the zoo. There's an emergency and your wife and all your sharpshooters have gone bowling! How soon can you get there?"

"Right away, Mr. Mayor," Buxton lied. "I'm just...er, waiting for my police car siren to get fixed."

"Forget the siren, you imbecile. Your men need you now!"

Goliath mind-projected to Reggie that there was a commotion going on down at the gates. Two stretch Cadillac limousines had arrived, one containing the mayor and the other with Flommock and Bernie Moon inside. Goliath stood in front of the gates, glaring at the limousines. No one was going to get past him.

"Honk your horn and maybe he'll move," Bernie Moon suggested.

"Are you nuts?" Flommock exclaimed. "He might charge at us and bite our heads off! I'm getting in the mayor's car!" Flommock slipped out of the driver's seat and hurried to the mayor's limo and climbed inside.

"You are a bumblehead, Max Flommock!" Throttlebottom said. "You don't even have the sense to buy a cellphone. I could strangle you! But we have more important things to do." The mayor fumbled with his phone and speed-dialed Plitt at the office building. "There's a Lion guarding the gates!"

"What do you expect me to do?" Plitt whined. "Bring him a pork chop with a birthday candle in it?"

"Don't get wise with me, Howard." Throttlebottom warned.

Plitt fumed. "Well, what can I do, Ralph? These animals have the place surrounded."

"Alright! Go and find that old zookeeper or that myopic little vet and tell them to move their Lion. Oh, never mind! I see they are already headed this way." Throttlebottom saw Reggie, Abby Sweet, and Dirk the Baboon walking briskly down the path towards the gates.

"Is that Bernie Moon I see in the maroon limo?" Abby Sweet asked Reggie.

"I do believe it is. Why do you suppose he has red smudges all over his face?"

"I don't know," she answered, "but I'm sure glad to see him." She opened the gates, gave Goliath a big smoochie kiss on his nose, then ran to the limo and gave Bernie Moon an even bigger smoochie on his lips.

"We've been trying to reach you for days, Bernie Moon!" she whined. "Reggie is on a hunger strike for better conditions for our animals. And the animals have broken out of their cages in a full-scale rebellion. Can you report this on TV?"

"You bet, Abby Sweet!' Bernie Moon gushed. "My camera crew is already on the way. I've been under cover. I'll tell you all about it later."

A police car, with siren blazing, arrived at the gates and skidded to a stop alongside the two limos. Police Chief Buxton jumped out and ran to the mayor's car. "Are you alright?" he asked.

"You'd better get inside. Don't you see that Lion over there?" Throttlebottom exclaimed. Buxton quickly jumped into the yellow limo. "I thought you said your siren was broken, Throttlebottom asked the Police Chief.

"Um, well, it got fixed," Buxton lied.

Reggie went over to Goliath and they walked together to the area behind the ticket booth. "Don't move until I tell you to," he told the Lion, "and then *Simba kunguruma*!"

"What does that mean?" Goliath asked.

"'Simba kunguruma' means *'Lion roar'* in the Swahili language of Africa," Reggie explained.

"Sorry, I don't speak Swahili. Only Lion," Goliath admitted.

Dirk the Baboon yowled a greeting in baboon-speak as he joined Reggie and Goliath. Together, the trio approached the mayor's yellow limo. Throttlebottom rolled down the window. "So, I see you're still alive and kicking, old timer," The mayor winked at Reggie.

"Barely, Mr. Mayor," gasped Reggie. "A hunger strike does have a tendency to sap one's energy."

"I suppose Flommock and I are now barred from the zoo while you and your animals destroy everything we have built?"

"On the contrary, sir," Reggie assured. "You and the president are most welcome to investigate this situation. I urge you to do so. Then we can sit down like two rational human animals and come to a settlement. But I must warn you, time is running out."

"Why should I negotiate with someone who has started a totally irresponsible fake riot?" Throttlebottom hissed.

Reggie took a deep breath. "Because it is your job as Chairman of the Board of the zoo to protect everyone on these premises from attack, and *that* includes your wife, who is currently with her lady friends in the bowling alley."

"Are you threatening my wife?" He turned to Flommock. "Did you hear him threaten my wife?"

"Gee, Ralph, I don't think so..."

"Aw, shut up! Let us in!" the mayor demanded of Reggie.

Reggie opened the gates for the mayor, the zoo president, and Chief of Police. "You may drive your vehicle very slowly to

## The Lincoln Zoo Rebellion

the office building," Reggie instructed. "And do not, I repeat, *DO NOT* park on any grass or run over any flowers!" He then closed his eyes and beamed a powerful mind-projection to all the animals, telling them to allow Throttlebottom's group safe passage. The yellow limo started up the path.

Reggie wondered if the Board of Directors and the mayor would come to their senses before he became too weak to carry on. Then he heard the call of small voices. "Reggie! Look at us!" He looked in the direction of the voices and saw a parade of children, dressed as fruit and vegetables, marching up Lincoln Road, shouting their slogans and waving their placards. He clapped his hands in delight.

"This is a brilliant demonstration, children! I am thrilled. We have a major rebellion going on here and we need intelligent, concerned kids like you to publicize our cause. The TV cameras will arrive soon, and you will lend a most colorful background to their report." He noticed a particular marching fruit.

"Excuse me. Didn't we once meet at a windy train station in Chicago?!" he asked the pineapple. The fruit's hands appeared and removed its head-mask and crown. It was Peter! Reggie hugged the boy enthusiastically, so pleased he was safe. Abby Sweet ran over and hugged him, too.

"Can we be on TV?" asked the carrot. "It's me, Little... uh, just Max. No more 'Little.'"

"Me too," shouted a head of celery, who Reggie immediately recognized as Bobby Winkleman.

"Ah, my dear boys," Reggie beamed. "I could sure use your help. You are the sons of important zoo officials and there is a major role you could play in this rebellion, if you're willing. Are you brave enough?"

"You bet!" they cried. "All of our friends will join us, too." Cory, Melly, LaToya, Scooter, and all the others echoed their agreement.

The camera crews from Channel Three TV arrived and quickly set up their equipment. Bernie Moon had scrubbed the lipstick and rouge from his face and removed the false eyelashes. He was now easy to identify as Bernie Moon.

With cameras rolling, and Reggie and Abby Sweet standing beside him, Bernie Moon motioned the children to hold up their signs. Then he raised a microphone to his mouth and made the first public announcement about the rebellion.

"Channel Three breaking news, Bernie Moon reporting. I am here at Lincoln Zoo, which will be closed until further notice. In the world's first animal rights protest of its kind, all of the zoo animals have escaped their defective cages and are running free, demanding better conditions. The rebellion is being led by retired zookeeper, Reggie Goodenough. Reggie, tell us what is happening."

Reggie cleared his throat and said rather weakly, "The animals and I are demanding better living conditions and more humane treatment. I have presented our demands to the executives of the zoo, but they have refused. We have nothing left to do but to go on strike…and I, myself, have begun a hunger strike. I will not eat or drink anything until our demands are met. I am pleased that I have the support of the most important people in Lincoln—these caring, wonderful children."

Peter, Little Max, Bobby, and the others cheered and held their signs high for the cameras to see.

## The Lincoln Zoo Rebellion

Reggie continued, "I call upon each and every one of you citizens of Lincoln to rally your friends and neighbors, sign petitions, and call your newspapers, radio and TV stations."

Reggie mind-beamed an order to Goliath to walk out slowly from behind the ticket booth over to Reggie. The children gasped and started to run in all directions.

"Don't go, children!" pleaded Reggie, ruffling the Lion's mane. "He won't hurt you. This is my close, personal friend, Goliath, and he will tell you how the animals feel about the situation at this zoo." He whispered in Goliath's ear, "Simba kunguruma."

The Lion and Reggie both opened their mouths and roared the loudest roar ever heard on television.

"Wow, that's some defiant roar! I'm Bernie Moon reporting for Channel Three and soon to be seen in the pages of the *Chicago Tribune*!"

The camera crew turned off their equipment and Bernie Moon handed the director his microphone. "Thanks boys. I'll stay here tonight and call you when there's anything new to report."

"We're going to make my cottage the base of operations," Reggie told Bernie Moon. "You're welcome to join us."

"That sounds great," answered the reporter. "Especially if your new vet is going to be there."

"You bet she is," Reggie replied. Then Peter, Max, Bobby, and Bernie Moon walked up the path towards the cottage accompanied by Sam the Giraffe, Lady Gaga, the Cheetah, Milt the Tiger, Louis the Lemur, and Goliath.

"Everyone inside!" Reggie ordered, as he opened his front door. "You will find two great-grandmothers who will fix you treats to eat. Please do not leave the cottage. I will proceed to the square alone for our very important strategy meeting with all the zoo's animals."

Back at the office building, Throttlebottom was having a conniption fit, shaking his hands above his head as he shouted at the Police Chief, "Buxton! What kind of cowardly, sissy, spineless cops do you have on that police 'farce' of yours?"

"I haven't been briefed yet, Mr. Mayor. Sorry," Buxton apologized.

"Briefed? What briefed? This is an emergency police action, you fool. So where are the cops? In a bowling alley with our wives, for goodness sake! Obviously, you can't handle it. I'd better call in some troops who can. Give me the phone!"

Throttlebottom placed an urgent call to Governor Handel B. Gladstone at the state capital. Because the mayor was an important political ally of the Governor, Gladstone immediately accepted the phone call. Throttlebottom passionately painted a grossly exaggerated picture of the rebellion at Lincoln Zoo, claiming that the animals were about to storm the city of Lincoln and were threatening the lives of women and children. He reminded the governor of his own generous contribution to Gladstone's last political campaign.

The Governor had no alternative but to declare an immediate state of emergency and call out the National Guard.

The National Guard brigade was dispatched within the hour. Tanks and troops carrying automatic weapons and light artillery rolled and marched out of headquarters and headed towards Lincoln. They were highly trained military men who had served in such foreign wars as Iraq and Afghanistan. It would take them nineteen hours to reach Lincoln, since the tanks were very slow.

Because this was an election year, Governor Gladstone thought it might help his campaign to go to Lincoln himself and show his leadership skills. He chartered a plane to fly him and his aides to this city that he was led to believe was on the verge of a major disaster.

"What will we do now, Ralph?" asked Winkleman.

"What should we do about our wives in the bowling alley?" asked Buxton.

"Nothing," declared the mayor. "We'll stay here all night, if need be, and wait until the National Guard troops arrive. Which should be around noon tomorrow."

Inside the bowling alley café, Holly Buxton and Libby Throttlebottom enjoyed their third glass of chardonnay. They, and other members of the Woman's Auxiliary bowling team, were unable to continue bowling, much to their annoyance. At least they could socialize and sip their drinks.

An unusual problem had been created by the pesky Penguins. Penguins have good eye-sight, but are not the smartest birds on the iceberg. Since they had never seen bowling pins before, and because the pins so closely resembled the shape of their own bodies, they were frightened that harm might come to this unfamiliar species of quiet penguins from the people rolling round rocks at them. So, when the women started to bowl, the Penguins ran down the alley and swept the pins away with their flippers before the balls could strike and hurt these stiff little cousins.

The police sharpshooters offered to shoot the Penguins, but the women wouldn't hear of it. "Those flipping Penguins are so cute! I think that one over there just fell in love with a bowling pin!" Holly Buxton laughed, cracking herself up. Seeing the impossibility of the situation, Holly suggested, "Let's have a few drinkies instead." The women headed for the bowling alley cocktail lounge.

## Chapter Seventeen

At the main square, Reggie stood with Fingers the Chimp and summoned all the animals to join him for their strategy meeting in front of the statue of Ralph Bear.

The Chimp told him, "There's something funny about that Bear."

"You're right," answered Reggie. I've never seen a spitting Bear either."

"No, it's something else I can't quite put my finger on," Fingers said.

Sigmund the Crocodile and Adolf the Alligator slithered up to Reggie, their great mouths suspiciously closed. Between them they had over 130 teeth.

"Open mouth!" Reggie ordered in a guttural squawk. They did so. Reggie checked out their open mouths to make sure neither had a penguin trapped inside. Satisfied that their mouths were penguin-free, Reggie commanded, "Shut mouth!" They obeyed. He patted them both on their heads. Those were the only words in Crocodile and Alligator he had mastered.

Emala, with a beautifully wound bandage on her shoulder, emerged from the veterinary surgery building, feeling much better after her operation and eager to join the meeting. The Aardvark, Thompson's Gazelle, and Okapi joined her. The Spider Monkeys danced up the path whistling their songs and wishing they could be swinging in trees.

Rambo the Hippo lumbered into the square as fast as his short legs would carry him and Sam the Giraffe arrived. When all of the animals had finally gathered, Reggie climbed up to the base of the Ralph Bear fountain and mind-beamed his thoughts to them.

He asked them to promise not to harm any humans and to report to him immediately if they felt there was any danger. He explained that the zoo must be cleared before sunset, with the exception of the zoo directors in the office building and the children at his cottage. That left only the Women's Auxiliary and police sharpshooters at the bowling alley.

## The Lincoln Zoo Rebellion

Fingers the Chimpanzee tapped Reggie on the shoulder and woofed out an idea. "I think we need a symbol of our rebellion."

"What did you have in mind?" Reggie asked.

"That so-called Bear," he said pointing to the statue. "It has to go."

"Go where?"

"Go to dust," clicked Fingers.

Reggie asked the other animals what they thought and they voiced their agreement with Fingers in a cacophony of grunts, howls, and assorted sounds. Before Reggie could object or further discuss the idea, Blomm came over and lifted Reggie onto his back and moved him out of harm's way. Rambo, the unusually large Hippo, took a running start and slammed into the Ralph Bear fountain. It wavered and Rambo hit it again. The Bear fountain toppled over and smashed to the ground, sending a twenty-foot stream of water jetting into the air.

Reggie called out to Fingers to shut off the water and told him where to find the water mains. The Chimp sprang into action and turned the mains off, cutting the flow to the spurting fountain. It took him some time, so puddles of water accumulated and the pathway turned muddy, much to the pleasure of Rambo and the Black Rhino, neither of whom had had a proper mud bath recently.

The zoo directors watched from the window. Throttlebottom choked back a sob when he saw his beloved Ralph Bear topple over. "That old codger is going to pay for this," he swore under his breath.

With Reggie on his back, Blomm removed tree trunks from the front of the bowling alley doors. He knelt down and, with one sweeping motion of his powerful trunk, safely placed Reggie on the ground. The zookeeper entered the bowling alley with Fingers, Emala and Dirk beside him and made an announcement: "Ladies and police, listen up! The animals and I will allow you safe passage to the gates so long as you leave your firearms behind and proceed slowly and make no threatening moves."

"How do we know the animals will not attack us?" Libby Throttlebottom asked, slurring her words thanks to having had a few too many cocktails.

"My men must carry their weapons," demanded the police captain.

"That is not possible," insisted Reggie. "This Elephant Blomm will not be controllable if he sees an exploding fire stick, and all of your lives will be at risk. Elephants are unable to jump, but they can certainly stomp, and I wouldn't bet against Blomm stomping all over you if you don't comply."

"Put down your weapons, men," the captain ordered.

"I will personally accompany you and I promise the animals will obey me," said Reggie, "but one threatening move and I will not be able to control them. I am weakened by my hunger strike, so you must do as I say."

Reggie mind-beamed orders to the animals to back off and he led the policemen and women to the gates without incident. The animals immediately moved away from the alley, opening up a wide pathway for the women and policemen, who were relieved by Reggie's control of the animals. The Penguins followed the large group of humans out of the bowling alley and accompanied them to the gates. Several of the birds had bowling pins tucked under their flippers, which they were stroking lovingly.

The zoo directors watched from the window of the office building. "Libby! Libby!" Throttlebottom called when he saw his wife, but she didn't hear him. A tear moistened each of his eyes in memory of his beloved Ralph Bear fountain.

The Black Rhino, covered in mud, trundled over to Reggie, and suggested that the office building was so flimsy, he could bring it down with a few good butts, if Reggie so desired.

"That will be unnecessary," the zookeeper told him, scratching the Rhino on the tender part of his forehead, "but you've given me an idea." He instructed the Rhino and Hippo to drag an empty cage into the square.

Reggie went back to his cottage, where he took a quick hot shower and changed into his best—and only—suit. He put on a bright blue necktie given to him by Tiny Teeny on his last birthday and gave a quick shine to his black shoes. He joined Max, Bobby, the two great-grandmothers, Bernie Moon, and Abby Sweet in the kitchen, where the vet laid out a spread of food.

"I am ready to begin negotiations with the Board of Directors, my friends," he said, "but I have a dreadful feeling that the mayor and his associates are still too stubborn to listen."

"Should we go with you?" Max suggested. "That would surprise my dad!"

Reggie thought about it for a moment. "I don't think so, my boy." I think you are more valuable here in hiding. But would you mind if I tell your fathers than you are being held captive by the animals?"

"That's a great idea!" Bobby Winkleman exclaimed. "Hostages, just like on TV!"

"Tell them we're about to be eaten!" giggled Max.

Reggie pondered this idea. "I think that would be too much of an exaggeration and I prefer to let them jump to their own conclusions. Would you be willing to write a little note pleading with them to meet the animals' demands?"

"Of course," the Devilish Duo agreed, and they started writing furiously.

Sadie had put her bag of dried apricots in a bowl on the table and she implored Reggie to eat a few and have some tea. "That will give you energy!"

"Pretty please!" tittered Tiny Teeny.

"I will not, my friends, and I really think the two of you should go back to the Bedside Manor Retirement Home for safety."

"We will not budge from this cottage," Tiny Teeny said firmly. "If you will not even take some food in support, at least let us give you moral support."

Bobby Winkleman chirped up, "Reggie, how will they know I really wrote this note? I don't think my dad would recognize my handwriting."

"That's a good point, Bobby," Reggie agreed. "It's a shame your hair is so short, or we could have sent a lock of it."

"How about my slingshot or yo-yo?"

"I'm afraid those objects do not really indicate you are in any danger."

Peter had a thunderbolt of an idea and whispered it in Max's ear.

Max laughed uproariously and yelled "Gimme five!" The boys slapped their hands together and Max opened his mouth so wide when laughing, that he snapped off the orange rubber bands on his braces and peeled off a loose bit of metal from his upper teeth.

"We'll send his braces," Peter cried, very pleased with himself.

"They were kinda loose anyway," Max added.

"I really don't like the idea of saying you've been kidnapped. But the lives of our animal friends are in grave danger. Desperate times require desperate deeds, I'm afraid. And this is a desperate time. We have to get their serious attention."

Sadie held out one of her dried apricots. "You could show him this and say it's one of the boys' ears!" Her intentions were good, even if the idea wasn't.

Reggie shook his head in disgust. "That's gross. And I don't think even those numbskulls would believe that!"

"Me neither," said Tiny Teeny. "I've got something infinitely better! Put this in your pocket," handing him a handkerchief. He slipped the hanky in his pocket without bothering to examine its contents.

Reggie walked to the office building with the Primates beside him. He straightened his blue necktie, took a deep breath, and opened the door to the office building and entered. He found his way to the meeting and, with Dirk and Fingers by his side, he took a deep breath as he stood in the doorway to the conference room, surveying the silent zoo directors and the Chief of Police with confidence.

"Gentlemen, I presume you are now prepared to come to an agreement," Reggie began. "The zoo has now been completely cleared by the animals. However, I must inform you that the animals have taken two young boys as hostages to encourage you to negotiate quickly. What'll it be?"

"You are asking us to believe the animals have taken hostages?" Plitt sputtered.

"Give them the notes, Dirk," Reggie told him in Baboon, and Dirk handed a note to Flommock.

"Oh no, Ralph! They've taken my son, Little Max."

"What a shame," Winkleman faked concern.

Then Dirk handed Winkleman a note, causing Winkleman's face to turn ashen white, and finally handed a note to Chief Buxton.

"Anyone could have written these notes," declared Buxton. "Are you sure it is your own son's handwriting?" he asked Flommock and Plitt. Neither man was positive.

"This will prove it to you," Reggie replied gesturing to Dirk. The Baboon leaned over the conference table so they could all see him and opened his hand, revealing Max's braces.

Flommock shrieked, Plitt gasped, and Winkleman felt sick. Dirk grunted and emitted a series of high-pitched squeals in satisfaction.

Reggie noted their reactions, then pressed on. "Allow me to translate the Baboon language for you. Dirk says if you do not agree to the animals' demands, they will be forced to remove the rest of the braces."

"You're bluffing and I don't buy it," jeered Throttlebottom.

"Fingers. Show him you are not bluffing."

The Chimp jumped up onto to the table hooting, clicking and stomping his feet. He held the handkerchief Tiny Teeny had given to Reggie. It was the hanky that Bernie Moon had used to wipe the red lipstick from his face. It was still gooey from all that red stuff and looked like drying blood. Dirk then slowly peeled away the edges of the hanky, revealing something that made them all gasp in horror.

There, in his good hand, he held Tiny Teeny's false teeth.

"My God!" cried Plitt. "First they take out Little Max's braces and now they've yanked Bobby's teeth!" Winkleman keeled over in a dead faint.

Flommock grabbed Throttlebottom by the lapels and shook him. "Ralph, stop this, Ralph. They're torturing our boys, Ralph!"

"Not at all, gentlemen." Reggie was as shocked as the mayor and his cronies at the teeth sitting in the open hanky. "These are obviously Tiny Teeny's false teeth…but I want you to realize that I can't tell you how far the animals will go if you don't agree to our terms," Reggie warned. "Who knows what will be next."

"I've had enough," the mayor growled, shoving Reggie away. "Your threats to harm little boys are idiotic and we don't care if you starve yourself to death."

At that moment, Reggie realized that any further talk was useless. The bewildered expressions on the faces of the other men brought Reggie to the conclusion they were too weak and frightened to stand up to Throttlebottom.

Suddenly, there was a tremendous crash as the Black Rhino burst through the front door of the office building. Covered in plaster, dry wall, and mud, he came lumbering into the conference room to tell Reggie that the spare cage had been moved into the square.

"Gentlemen," Reggie addressed the directors and Chief of Police. "Our Black Rhino here has come to the conclusion that these offices are not secure enough. He insists that you should be moved into a cage outside until an agreement can be reached. Otherwise, he will bring the building down on top of you."

"All right," Throttlebottom sighed. "We'll get into your stupid cage. It won't be for long anyway. Help will be here soon, and *you* will be toast."

Chief Buxton slung Winkleman over one shoulder and they marched out through the broken door and into the square, followed by Reggie, Dirk, Fingers, and the Black Rhino.

Durante the Proboscis Monkey held the cage door open and hooted "There ya go, there ya go…" as each of the men climbed over the smashed rubble that had been Ralph Bear and entered the cage. As soon as the prisoners were inside, the Primates slammed it shut and secured it with a padlock.

"Now you will see what it is actually like to be a zoo animal," Reggie said softly, his energy diminishing. "If I can survive my hunger strike one more night, I will return tomorrow morning to see if you are ready to negotiate. The animals are willing to listen to any offer from you that will give them a better quality of life. Good night and sweet dreams. Luckily it's a warm evening, so you will not freeze to death."

"Can we have a TV?" asked Flommock.

"No," Reggie replied.

"How about a book or newspaper?" asked Winkleman.

"Sorry."

"But we're going to starve," whined Throttlebottom.

"No you won't," Reggie promised. "We have ordered you Impossible Burgers from the Small Planet Coffee Shop."

"What's impossible about them?" asked Buxton.

"They are plant-based and meat-free," Reggie answered. "No animal was harmed, no climate warmed, no fossil fuel burned, and I'll bet you won't even be able tell the difference."

Bernie Moon summoned his camera crew who returned to the zoo for his latest update on the ten o'clock news:

## The Lincoln Zoo Rebellion

"Breaking news about the Lincoln Zoo animal negotiations. There you have it, folks. The Board of Directors, including our mayor and Chief of Police, have been locked in a cage in the main square by a couple of Monkeys. Despite the animals taking two little boys as hostages, they refuse to negotiate an agreement. And, tragically, our beloved zookeeper Reggie Goodenough is in the fifth day of a hunger strike and may not have long to live.

"What can you, the public, do about it? Pick up your phones and send e-mails to the Governor or, yes, even the Congress of the USA. Get mad! This is Bernie Moon, Channel Three News, live from Lincoln Zoo."

The camera panned past Bernie Moon and up the path to show animals of every species dancing and prancing with pride. It zoomed in on the zoo directors and Police Chief clinging to the bars of the cage, with Winkleman prostrate on the floor. The mayor was seen to gulp from a flask, which, of course, contained mouthwash, which he spit out through the bars.

In his chartered airplane, Governor Handel B. Gladstone switched off his portable television set. "What's with that mayor anyway?" he asked an aide. "Was he gulping and spitting whiskey? It doesn't look to me like those animals are about to storm the town. They're dancing up a storm right there at the zoo. But they don't look that dangerous."

"This rebellion could be great publicity for you," explained the aide. "It might even get you the vice-presidential nomination!"

"I hope so. Gee I hope that old zookeeper is going to be okay. I used to hear a lot of great things about him from my kids back when we lived in Lincoln."

## Chapter Eighteen

At dawn, the National Guard tanks rumbled along on their way to Lincoln, accompanied by troop trucks carrying soldiers. Approaching Lincoln from the north, they continued to pass over the mountain road into Horace Heights and then down the hills into the suburb of Rudy Valley and across Clint East Woods. Their commander was prepared for any eventuality. "I hope there's real trouble so I can git a Tiger in my gun sights," he told his lieutenant. "I always wanted a Tiger-skin rug."

The morning edition of the *Lincoln Examiner* made no mention whatsoever of the situation at the zoo, of course, but that didn't matter. Few people in Lincoln were reading the paper because it had become so boring, being filled with nothing but ads and stories about Throttlebottom's toy store.

However, almost everyone in town had watched Bernie Moon's television news reports on both the 6:00 p.m. and 10:00 p.m. news. That publicity had inspired thousands of people to drive to the zoo that morning to try to catch sight of rebelling animals. They were warned to stay in their cars, as a safety measure.

Traffic virtually came to a halt along Lincoln Zoo Road. Police helicopters hovered overhead, their pilots blaring out loudspeaker announcements imploring the motorists to return home. But they were ignored.

After a fitful night's sleep on the floor of the cage, the zoo directors' bodies were stiff and achy. The Spider Monkeys brought them water and, for breakfast, a whole stalk of bananas. Dirk handed Mayor Throttlebottom a note through the bars. The mayor read it, tore it up, and threw the scraps back at the Baboon. The note was from Reggie. "When you are ready to negotiate, just shake your head 'yes' at Dirk here and he will come fetch me."

The National Guard convoy arrived at Veronica Lake and took a break. The soldiers were allowed thirty minutes by the commander to eat breakfast.

"Can you shoot a Tiger without a hunting permit?" the lieutenant asked the commander.

"Why not? We're on an official military action. Anything in the way is fair game!"

After littering the area with plastic coffee cups and paper plates, the soldiers set off once again. The tanks were hard on the pavement and the ground around the road as they turned down DiCaprio Road and headed towards Ankle Avenue, Lincoln Station. and town.

In the living room of Reggie's cottage, Bernie Moon closed his cellphone with a long, sad face and put his hand on the zookeeper's shoulder, which was bonier than it had ever been. "Bad news, my friend. My editor at the TV station tells me the governor has called out the National Guard."

"Ah," sighed Reggie wearily. "No wonder Throttlebottom refuses to negotiate. Once the National Guard arrives with their guns and artillery, we shall have to give up."

"Could we create a diversion?" asked Peter.

"I'm afraid not," Reggie sighed. "I think we have run out of options. If the governor has called out the military, it must mean he supports our furshlugginer mayor."

Bernie Moon scratched his curly round head of hair. "Not necessarily. I could ask him. He's here in Lincoln."

"The governor is here? Now?" Reggie asked, surprised.

"He flew in last night. He's staying at the local motel, walking distance from the zoo."

Reggie's eyes began to shine once again. "Excellent! That's something your children's committee can do right away! Take all your friends down to the motel with your signs and persuade the governor to come to the zoo immediately. There is no time to waste. If the governor gets here before the National Guard arrives, we might have a chance."

"We won't take 'no' for an answer, Reggie," promised Peter and the three boys ran from the cottage.

Reggie called after them, "Don't let anyone see you! You're supposed to be hostages!" Max and Bobby retrieved their carrot and celery outfits from the ticket booth and Peter put on his pineapple costume.

The group of vegetable-disguised kids ran along Lincoln Zoo Road towards town. They were amazed to see the traffic jam with so many cars filled with people interested in seeing what was going on at the zoo. They spotted some of their friends, including Cory, Scooter, Jaime, LaToya, Melly and several others.

"C'mon with us!" yelled Peter. "We're going to see the governor!" The children jumped out of their parents' cars and joined the boys. Peter tossed them the sack filled with lots of the harvest festival vegetable and fruit costumes.

Just past Plitt's gas station, the National Guard convoy had run into a traffic jam along Lincoln Zoo Road and they were stuck. The commander got out his survey maps, but they were uselessly out of date because so much construction had recently occurred in town.

The commander stopped an old man on the street and asked directions. "Is there a back way to the zoo?"

The old man sent them on a route that took them northeast, through a trailer park and past some new office buildings. The tanks knocked down fences of a housing development and one tank got stuck in somebody's swimming pool.

Governor Handel Gladstone and his aides met in the breakfast room of the motel to figure out what to do. They had heard radio reports of the terrible traffic jams on Lincoln Zoo

Road. "We don't have enough facts," pointed out one of the aides. "How can we obtain more facts?"

"Why don't we set up a fact-finding committee?" asked another.

"Right," agreed a third. "They can start by finding out what special interest groups are involved, and who stands to gain what, how much, and when."

The governor and the group heard a loud commotion of young voices outside and went to investigate. The sight was impressive. Nearly every child in town had gathered, chanting protests and holding up signs. Many were dressed in colorful fruit and vegetable costumes.

"This is incredible," the governor said. "I haven't seen a demonstration like this since the Equal Rights Amendment march!"

Max took off his carrot head and yelled, "In this town, sir, E.R.A. stands for 'Equal Rights for Animals!'"

Bobby Winkleman cried out, "We need your help, governor. The only way to stop the rebellion at the zoo is for you to get there before the National Guard troops.

Gladstone turned to his aides. "These kids are right. There isn't time for fact-finding committees. Let's get over to the zoo and see what's going down."

"How can we do that, Sir?" asked an aide. "The radio says there are traffic jams everywhere."

"We can walk together!" Peter cried. "It's not far."

"You can ride in my scooter!" Scooter Goldfarb offered.

"I can happily walk," answered the governor, smiling his best political smile.

Gladstone and his aides followed the children back to the zoo. Along the way he shook hands with many people stuck in the traffic jam who told him how important the zoo was to them. And he also talked to the children, including the Devilish Duo and Peter, who told him what a great inspiration Reggie had been to them.

"Reggie Goodenough. Yes! I remember my kids talking about him," the governor exclaimed. "He used to give them a cookie called a snickerdoodle! They persuaded me to send him a little gift for his retirement."

The National Guard tanks finally arrived, and easily crashed through the barbed wire fence on the grounds of the zoo. Leslie Wolf and the Spotted Hyena were the first to see them, and off they ran to Reggie's cottage as fast as they could to report.

Reggie listened to the Wolf and Hyena. "We've lost," he sadly told Abby Sweet, Bernie Moon, and the great-grandmothers. "I will mind-beam orders to send all the animals back to their cages now. Our rebellion is over."

He stepped outside and beamed the retreat order to the animals. Tails between their legs—those with tails—and all others, each and every one, obeyed him and returned to their cages. Goliath, moving very glumly, swaying to and fro as he ambled up the path, passed Bernie Moon running in the opposite direction to the gates to file his first unpleasant news report of the day.

"Breaking news," Bernie Moon exclaimed sharply into the camera. "The National Guard has stormed the fences of Lincoln Zoo. All of the animals have returned to their cages. It appears their rebellion has ended. The crisis is over.

## The Lincoln Zoo Rebellion

"But Reggie Goodenough, the popular old zookeeper, is still alive," he continued, "But the end may be soon. It can now be revealed that he possesses a talent that he has kept secret for many years. He has learned to speak many of the animals' own languages, which is the reason that they have so willingly obeyed his orders. This is Bernie Moon, channel three news, live from the Lincoln Zoo."

The National Guard commander and his men skirted the playground and swimming pool, their AR-15 automatic rifles at the ready. Each cage they passed had a peaceful animal in it, resting and pretending to be asleep. Goliath snored loudly. "I don't get it, commander," said the lieutenant. "I thought there was a riot going on here?"

They marched into the quiet square and halted, gazing at the cage that held the Board of Directors.

"What took you so long?" Throttlebottom yelled. "We've been waiting here all night."

"Tanks ain't jet airplanes, are they, bub?" the commander cracked.

"Well, anyway, you're finally here. So let us out of this cage right this minute."

"Where's the key?" the commander asked.

"If we had a key, we'd be outa here already, you dimwit," the mayor growled.

"Why don't you shoot off the lock, commander?" Flommock suggested.

"Too dangerous. Bullets could ricochet and hit one of you. Find me some chains, lieutenant? We'll attach them to the bars and have the tanks rip 'em off."

The lieutenant apologized that, unfortunately, all the chains and grappling hooks were in the tool compartment of the tank that had become stuck in the swimming pool two miles to the north. He sent a squad of National Guardsmen to recover them.

Finally, Governor Gladstone and the children arrived at the gates. The governor spotted Bernie Moon.

"Hi, Moon. I've seen you on TV. You're a pretty darned good reporter. What exactly is going on here?" Bernie Moon gave the Governor his view of the situation as the two men walked together up the path towards the square.

"I think an official State Hearing is in order," Governor said, but he declined Bernie Moon's request to let his camera crew televise the hearing live.

Peter removed his pineapple costume and headed towards the ticket booth to hide it away and put on his Ed Sheeran T-shirt. Suddenly, he was grabbed from behind and spun around.

"There you are!" the man yelled triumphantly in his face, holding his Rhino horn dagger at Peter's throat. "I am Edward Eugene Pincus of Immigration and Customs Enforcement, known as ICE, and you are under arrest for being an illegal African alien." Pincus slapped handcuffs on Peter's wrists and marched him up the path towards the square.

Max and Bobby Winkleman saw Peter being manhandled by Pincus and followed them. "He's with us!" Max shouted. "Let him go!" but Pincus ignored their pleas.

Governor Gladstone ordered the National Guard commander to set up a table and chairs in front of the cage holding the zoo directors. He refused Throttlebottom's demand to speak to him in private. "I don't see why we can't have our official State

Hearing right here, Mr. Mayor. After all, it's a beautiful summer's day." The mayor fumed.

The Governor sent the National Guard lieutenant to fetch Reggie. The old zookeeper arrived at the square dressed in a freshly laundered khaki zookeeper outfit and his ever-present toolbox. He looked worn out and skinny. Abby Sweet, Bernie Moon, Bobby, Max and the great-grandmothers walked with him, arm-in-arm.

Flommock and Winkleman suddenly spotted their sons from the cage. "Maxie, Maxie, how's your poor teeth?" Flommock asked his son.

"Bobby? Are you all right, son?" Winkleman asked. Both boys grinned, their wide smiles showing that their mouths were intact, teeth and all.

"I think we've been bamboozled," Plitt said angrily.

Officer Pincus held on to Peter and the National Guard troops stood at attention as they all recited the Pledge of Allegiance. The governor gave the mayor the first opportunity to speak.

Throttlebottom ranted and raved, accusing the zookeeper of menacing the lives of everyone in Lincoln with dangerous beasts and claimed that Reggie's ability to speak to animals could have led to mass hysteria. He stated that everyone in town backed his decision to provide more fun amusement attractions instead of boring animals. Then he demanded that the governor throw Reggie in jail for inciting a riot.

"What do you have to say to the mayor's remarks?" asked the Governor.

Reggie stood up weakly. The great-grandmothers gave him a round of applause, but they had gloves on their hands, so it just sounded like the flapping of birds' wings.

Reggie cleared his throat and began. "Mr. Governor, distinguished military guests, friends and foes. I was tempted to stand here today and reveal a history of bribery, corruption, embezzlement, deception, stock manipulation, insurance fraud and, worst of all, violation of the first amendment to the Constitution of the United States: free speech and freedom of the press."

"Ralph, what is he talking about?" Flommock asked the mayor.

"He's senile," Throttlebottom grunted, sweating visibly. "Don't worry, no one is listening."

Reggie cleared his throat and took a deep breath. "I believe that keeping animals in cages is cruel and unjust. They will be happier and healthier in natural environments. We have the space. I have translated our animals' desires into English and presented them to the Board of Directors of the zoo, but they refuse to listen.

"I beg you to consider the plight of animals around the world. Their homes are being stolen by developers. Forest fires, hurricanes, earthquakes, tsunamis, floods, and crazy weather extremes caused by global warming are pushing animals to the brink of extinction.

"That's why good zoos and wild animal parks are vitally important. They are refuges that save declining species. Here we have a place where we can allow animals to be animals again. We can restore their pride and then either return them to their natural environments or make those environments here.

"I'm sure that if we can't get it right in this little zoo in Lincoln, we have no chance of getting it right in our state, country, or the world.

## The Lincoln Zoo Rebellion

"Our zoo could become a truly fabulous wild animal preserve. It is half destroyed as it is now. You have the choice of rebuilding it in a way that can fulfill its potential to become a sanctuary for animals that will do more for your children's humanity in the long run than any waterpark or games arcade can do."

The governor stood up and addressed Reggie. "My dear fellow. It is clear that the Board of Directors of this zoo were only interested in exploiting animals to build their money-making amusement facility. You, however, were willing to die for them with your hunger strike. But the mayor maintains that he has the support of the people. I am at a loss to make a judgment in this matter."

"But he doesn't have the support of the people," Max spoke up. "I have a signed petition by every child in Lincoln saying we want this zoo to become just like Reggie says it should be. And their parents agree!" He thrust the petition in front of the governor.

"The mayor *does not* have the support of the adults, Mr. Governor," Bernie Moon declared. "My television station received over two thousand calls last night alone, pledging support to Reggie."

The Governor nodded in agreement. "That settles it then," the Governor addressed the entire group, after pausing for dramatic effect. He then announced loudly, "By the power vested in me by this state, I hereby proclaim..." He stopped and thought a moment. "But wait a minute. Is this zoo on city or state property?" The Governor's aides huddled together, frantically flipping through their cell phones and chattering among themselves. Finally, one aide sidled over to the governor, cupped his hand over the governor's ear and whispered something.

"Oh, my goodness," the Governor shook his head. "I guess we really don't have any power here. These lands evidently belong to the city."

"I beg to differ with you, Mr. Governor," Reggie corrected. "These lands were purchased with the zoo taxes paid or contributed by the people of Lincoln. By definition, the zoo belongs to them, the people." Every human and animal looked surprised, then glanced back and forth at one another, looking for reaction.

"Excellent!" The governor turned to Throttlebottom. "Mr. Mayor, do you wish us to verify proof of the people's desires, which would mean setting up a committee with a few criminal lawyer associates of mine to dig deep?"

Throttlebottom looked defeated. "That won't be necessary, Governor. Though I feel I'm right, I will be resigning my positions both as Chairman of the Board of this zoo and mayor to spend more quality time with my family and business."

Excellent!" the Governor crowed. "I am very pleased to have been the man to settle this rebellion. Is there any other business? I must get back to the state capital."

"Yes, there is, Mr. Governor," Pincus spoke up. "I am with ICE and I wish to announce that I have caught and arrested this here undocumented illegal alien, Peter Nelson N'gara, and I'm going to put him on a plane back to Africa!"

Wait!" Reggie held the palm of his hand up to Pincus' face. He turned his head to the governor and pleaded. "Sir, I implore you to listen for one more minute. Peter came to this country on a ship from Africa, dressed as a pineapple, to escape persecution and threats of imprisonment by a corrupt African regime that has already put his innocent parents in jail. I will happily vouch for him, in the name of justice. I'll even adopt him, if that's what it takes. Please allow him to stay, sir."

"Remove the handcuffs, Pincus," commanded the governor. We don't deport pineapples from this country. Especially African pineapples. The boy is free to stay in America." Pincus obeyed the governor's order and Peter ran to hug Reggie with grateful tears in his eyes.

The Governor turned to Reggie, and quietly said, "You don't need to adopt. But if you'll sponsor him, that'd be great. This boy deserves the fine home and life I know you will give him." Then the governor leaned closer to Reggie, pointed to the cage, and whispered, "By the way, do you have the key to let them out of that cage?"

"Oh, we don't need a key," Reggie answered. He took a small hammer out of his toolbox, walked over to the cage and tapped the end bar gently. The bars along one side collapsed, clanging to the ground.

"This cage is as faulty as all the rest of them," Reggie said with a smug smile. "They could have walked out any time they wanted."

Throttlebottom, his right eye twitching angrily, stepped out of the cage, his head hanging in shame and walked off down the path, alone.

"I think that does it," the Governor announced, then paused. "Ah, no, there is one more thing. By the power which hasn't really been vested in me…but I don't think the people of Lincoln or its elected officials would object to…I hereby appoint Reggie Goodenough to the job of Chief Operating Officer of Lincoln Zoo for as long as he wishes to occupy the position." Animals and humans alike filled the air with a joyous burst of vocal sounds, clapping hands, clacking hooves, flapping wings, and much, much more to express their joy.

When the celebration calmed down, Reggie summoned his last weakened ounce of strength to declare "I humbly accept, Mr. Governor."

"And furthermore," Gladstone announced, "I will turn over to Reggie my special development fund for major development projects my office considers to be the highest priority in this state."

"I am speechless!" exclaimed the zookeeper. "That is the biggest surprise of all!"

The Governor spoke confidentially in Reggie's ear. "By the way, did you ever get that hundred-dollar bill I sent to you after your retirement? My children wanted me to do it."

"That was you? There was no note. I have often wondered who sent it!" Reggie exclaimed. "How can I thank you?"

"Name the first animal born in this zoo after me," the Governor suggested.

"That's a promise!" Reggie raised his arms to the skies and beamed a mind-projection of absolute victory to the animals. An enormous collective roar pierced the air, and they slowly and cautiously left their cages and joined the celebration in the square. They circled around Reggie, expressing animal words and mind projections of joy and gratitude.

Blomm lifted Reggie, Abby Sweet and Peter on to his back and Reggie called down to Bernie Moon. "Hey, Bernie! Shall we announce our victory to the world?"

"You bet!" cried the reporter as he hurried towards the gates to organize his camera crew.

## The Lincoln Zoo Rebellion

The Black Rhino spied Officer Pincus sitting in the rubble of the Ralph Bear fountain. He was picking his fingernails with the ornately carved Rhino horn dagger. Blowing a monstrous snort of air through his nostrils, the Rhino abruptly turned, lowered his head and charged. His long front horn caught the ICE man under the seat of his pants and sent Pincus sailing into the air. "Ohhhhhhhh!" He landed head-first in a gigantic pile of Hippo manure.

His was the only minor injury in the otherwise nonviolent riot at Lincoln Zoo.

Waiting anxiously for Reggie and the animals at the gates, all the children of Lincoln—dressed in fruit and vegetable outfits—began chanting "Reggie, Reggie, Reggie!" The cameras rolled, the crowd cheered, and Bernie Moon announced the animals' victory.

From Blomm's broad back, Reggie surveyed the scene below. He was delighted by the children's enthusiasm. As he looked back over his shoulder, he realized that he was seeing Lincoln Zoo in its present, sad state for the last time. Tomorrow he would start to rebuild it—his way.

In the traffic jam out on Lincoln Zoo Road he spotted a truck, stopped, unable to move. It was Calhoun's Critter Cages with a new load of faulty gleaming metal cages. "Go back home, Calhoun!" Reggie shouted. "We will never need your shoddy goods again!"

Max called from the ground, "Can I come up there too?"

Blomm reached down and lifted up the boy so he was face-to-face with Reggie. They shook hands. "Are you going to eat my mushroom soup now?" Max asked.

Reggie nodded, smiling. "You bet your sweet life, Max. I can't wait! By the way, I'm not calling you and Bobby "the Devilish Duo" anymore. You are now "the Dynamic Duo!'"

Max beamed. "You're my hero, Reggie. I'll never let you down."

The Lincoln Zoo rebellion had come to an end. But the celebration had only just begun.

# Epilogue

Only one year has passed since the end of the animals' rebellion at Lincoln Zoo, but already an amazing transformation has taken place.

Needless to say, there is not a single cage to be seen. All the amusement games and rides are gone. The office building was razed to the ground and the toy store has been turned into a library, reading room, and crafts center. The bowling alley is now a free theatre showing wildlife documentary films from morning until night.

The barbed wire fences are gone, of course, replaced by twelve-foot-high hedges, the tops of which are shaped into heads of animals—thanks to a very clever gardener-sculptor.

Reggie has divided the zoo into five major areas he named, "The Five A's and E." That stands for *Americas, Asia, Africa, Antarctica, and Australia.* Plus Europe. Each "A" and the "E" contains animal species native to that specific continent. African animals, for instance, aren't permitted into the Australia section and vice versa. Each continent has a watering hole or two, a small lake, artificial hills for the climbers, and plenty of trees and flowers. They even have separate reptile houses, so you won't see a Python from Asia next to a Rattlesnake or Anaconda from the Americas or a King Brown from Australia. The Penguins love Antarctica. Many of them were allowed to keep their own personal bowling pin.

With the exception of poisonous reptiles, most animals have the run of their particular continent. Each of them has also been provided with natural habitats that Reggie designed together with the individual animals.

While the zoo is open during the day, most animals prefer staying in their habitats rather than wander around. At night, however, after the zoo is closed, they can roam freely and forage for the food that the new employees hide for them. There has never been an accident.

Visitors now drive around the zoo in safe, enclosed electric golf carts, driven by members of the Senior Citizen Harley Davidson Motorcycle Club, and supervised by their leader Jovino

Matzos. The carts in 'Africa' are painted with Zebra stripes, while the 'Australian' ones resemble Kangaroos. Small children can ride in the 'pouches' provided on the Kangaroo carriers. Reggie is hoping that one day he can raise funds to build a monorail, so visitors will be off the ground completely.

When school started in the fall and many of the student employees had to leave, Reggie hired a number of elderly retired people. Now the snack stands are manned mostly by grandmothers and grandfathers. Sadie and Tiny Teeny sit in the ticket booth and give free snickerdoodles to everyone who buys a ticket. The Bedside Manor Retirement Home is almost completely deserted during the day.

New animals have been arriving regularly and it was a particularly joyous occasion when mates arrived for Fingers and Dirk. Coincidentally, Fingers' new partner turned out to be the most attractive female from his own Pygmy Chimpanzee troop in Africa. They swung together for hours, talking about old times and old friends.

The best news is that Emala is pregnant. An Eastern Lowland Silverback Gorilla named Elvis was loaned to Lincoln Zoo by the marvelous San Diego Zoo and Wild Animal Park in Southern California and, according to Reggie, she is hoping for a boy. Reggie hopes so too, so he can name it Handel after both the Governor and one of his favorite classical music composers.

There have been a number of changes in town, as well. The major one is that the toy factory closed down forever. After the excitement of the Lincoln Zoo rebellion, Bernie Moon broke the story he had been researching when he masqueraded as a female Willy Wombat toy stuffer. It hit the front page of the

*Chicago Tribune* and many other newspapers around America. The headline read:

## TOY COMPANY STUFFS ANIMALS WITH NOXIOUS CHEMICALS

The Japanese canceled their order. Millions of Ralph Bears and Willy Wombats were recalled because of the toxic stuffing materials causing pollution. The usual five o'clock yellow cloud of smoggy haze over Lincoln disappeared. Hospital visits by people suffering with asthma and emphysema were reduced by more than half.

Throttlebottom went bankrupt and had to sell his interest in the *Examiner* to pay the taxes and his fines for crimes against the environment. He also had to sell his fake castle. His wife Libby's nephew bought it and is building a waterpark on the property with a video games arcade twice as large as the one Blomm destroyed at the zoo.

Max Flommock got straight A's in the autumn term at Barack Obama Middle School. His braces are off, and his delicious mushroom soup was so well received by Reggie and the great-grandmothers that he is thinking of becoming a chef. Bobby Winkleman, who now wishes to be called Robert, sports long hair over his ears, which his father hates, and his voice has changed to a deep baritone.

For a class assignment, Peter wrote a story about the Lincoln Zoo Rebellion and praised the participation of Max, Robert, and the other children who played such a significant role. Peter's manuscript won first prize at the school's English writing contest. Max, Robert, and the other children meet up often with Peter at

## The Lincoln Zoo Rebellion

the zoo to reminisce about the time they helped end the rebellion.

Romance is in the air. Max has two girlfriends, Robert has three, and Peter has gone on his first date with LaToya Tricklebank to see Disney's latest blockbuster movie, "The Lincoln Zoo Rebellion."

Abby Sweet and Bernie Moon's wedding is set for next month. Reggie, of course, will be Bernie's best man. Reggie himself is seeing a lot of Emma Jean Likorisch at the Small Planet Coffee Shop, who will be Abby Sweet's maid of honor at the big wedding.

Reggie is in constant touch with Governor Gladstone, who played an important fund-raising role in the re-building of the zoo. Gladstone is on the ticket to become vice president of the USA, and he asked the zookeeper if he'd be interested in a post with the Environmental Protection Agency, should he be elected.

"I'm too busy for that, my good man," Reggie told him. "With the zoo and Bernie Moon and my new TV show, I just don't have the time!" Their weekly local TV show, "Talking with Animals," features a new animal each week. Lady Gaga was their first guest. Goliath is a regular on the program, and it is a major hit. There is talk of it going national on PBS.

Peter's parents were found! When Joe Otoronga was illegally arrested, he was taken to the same jail that held the couple. With the help of a few Bushbaby and Marmoset friends, they escaped and made their way back to Mbinguni, Central Africa. Of course, Jobi Conn O'Brien gave them refuge in the game reserve. Imagine their surprise to discover that their son Peter was in America!

A few weeks later the dictator was deposed, and the N'garas were able to return to their own home. They e-mailed the zoo asking Peter to return to Africa.

Peter sent back this e-mail:

*Dearest mother and father. I jumped for joy when I heard the great news!*

*I have missed you so much and I think about you all the time.*

*I am healthy and very busy as I am attending Lincoln Middle School and helping out a zookeeper named Reggie and some wonderful animals that I adore.*

*I have many close friends. I have applied to become a citizen of the USA and I hope someday to be a veterinarian.*

*Would you consider becoming an African-American family together? I hope and pray you will say yes.*

*Your loving son, Peter.*

Peter's parents, Seko N'gara and his wife Lakeisha, placed a long-distance telephone call to Peter at the zoo and they had a happy, tearful reunion. Reggie got on the line and offered Mr. N'gara the position of Head of Marketing and Sales for the zoo.

When his parents arrived in Lincoln, they immediately took a cab to the zoo. Reggie and Peter met them with hugs, kisses, and smiles, and then walked hand-in-hand with them to the new square and fountain. The shattered Ralph Bear had been replaced with a new statue that represents the dignity that should be shared by animals and humans: a statue of Reggie, with Goliath by his side, and a shooting water display illuminated by thousands of colored lights. It was donated by friends of the Governor.

Reggie often takes a handkerchief from the pocket of his khakis and polishes the engraved brass plaque at the base of his statue, a plaque which reminds all visitors to the zoo that the land on which they walk belongs first to the animals.

## Cast of Characters

Reggie Goodenough: The old zookeeper of The Lincoln Zoo, who can communicate and mind-speak in many animal languages.

Goliath, the Lion: Good friend of Reggie.

Little Max Flommock: One of the two "Devilish Duo" kids

Big Max Flommock: father of Little Max. Owns "Big Max's Used Car Lot" and is President of the zoo's Board of Directors.

Bobby Winkleman: The other kid of the "Devilish Duo."

Bill Winkleman Jr.: Bobby's father, who just opened his third grocery store and is Vice President of the zoo's Board of Directors.

Bill Winkleman: Bobby's grandfather, who opened the first grocery store in Lincoln.

Ralph Throttlebottom: Owner of Throttlebottom's Toys, and Mayor of Lincoln. He's the new owner of the zoo and is the Chairman of the zoo's Board of Directors.

"Ralph Bear": The hot-selling toy bear named after Ralph Throttlebottom.

Howard Plitt: Works at new gas station; is Secretary-Treasurer of zoo's Board of Directors.

Abby Sweet: The zoo's new, cute, inexpensive veterinarian.

Sadie Teeny and Tiny Teeny: Two elderly lady friends of Reggie.

Hugh, the Canadian Red Fox: Taught Reggie his first animal "mind language."

Emala, the Gorilla: A female lowland Gorilla

Fingers, the Chimpanzee

Milt, the Tiger

Leslie, the Wolf

Cosmo, the Flamingo

Louie, the Ring-tailed Lemur

Adolf, the Crocodile

Sigmund, the Alligator

Rambo, the Hippo

Sam, the Giraffe

Blomm, the African Elephant

Lyle, the Lynx

Lady Gaga, the Leopard

The Cheetah, Black Rhino, Baboon, and Penguins

Schoolkids: Jaime Gutierrez, LaToya Tricklebank, Melly Belloso, Scooter Goldfarb, and Cory Chang, the kid who rode a skunk and couldn't get rid of the smell.

"Jobi" Conn O'Brien: An ex-animal tracker who now runs an animal wildlife preserve in Central Africa ("Jobi" means "boss" in Swahili).

Joe Otoronga: Jobi Conn's number one man.

Kafi, Evaristo, and Mitch: African helpers of "Jobi" Conn O'Brien and Joe Otoronga.

Peter Nelson N'gara: Thirteen-year-old African teenager, who escaped persecution by an African tyrant by hiding on a ship carrying animals from Africa to the Lincoln Zoo.

Zick Wineapple: Postman in Lincoln.

Grant Buxton: Lincoln's Chief of Police.

Harold G. Koonin: Canadian Banker who heads the Lincoln Examiner newspaper syndicate.

Governor Handel B. Gladstone: Governor of the state.

# Now Available!

## AWARD-WINNING AUTHOR
## NADINE HARUNI

## The Secret Life of Ryan Rigbee
### The Hat Diaries
### Book One

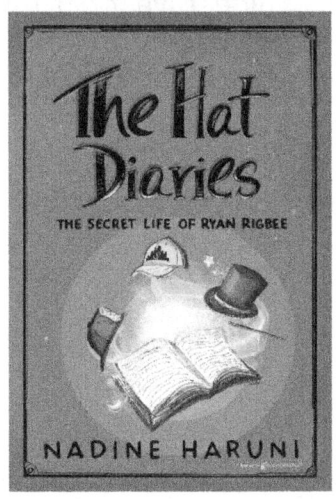

**THE HAT DIARIES™ *The Secret Life of Ryan Rigbee*** is the debut novel in **THE HAT DIARIES™** middle-grade fantasy trilogy and marks the start of a coming-of-age story resonating with readers of all ages. This imaginative, action-packed novel follows a teen struggling with loss, love, bullying, and loneliness.

**For more information
visit:** www.SpeakingVolumes.us